DIAMOND STREET

THE STORY OF THE LITTLE TOWN WITH THE BIG RED LIGHT DISTRICT

BRUCE EDWARD HALL

BLACK · DOME

BLACK DOME PRESS CORP.
RR1, Box 422
Hensonville, NY 12439
518-734-6357

First Edition, 1994

Published by Black Dome Press Corp.
RR1, Box 422
Hensonville, NY 12439
518-734-6357

Library of Congress Cataloging-in-Publication Data
Hall, Bruce Edward.
    Diamond Street: the story of the little town with the big red light
district/Bruce Edward Hall.
        p. cm.
    ISBN 1-883789-01-X
    1. Prostitution—New York (State)—Hudson—History. 2.
Hudson (N.Y.)—History. 3. Hudson (N.Y.)—Social life and customs.
4. Police corruption—New York (State)—Hudson—History.
5. Political corruption—New York (State)—Hudson—History.
I. Title
HQ146.H84H34   1994
974.7'39—dc20   94-25090
                                                       CIP

Design by Carol Clement, Artemisia, Inc.

Printed in the USA

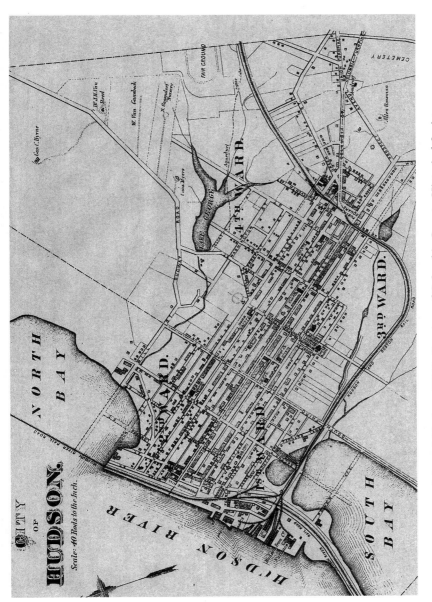

Map of Hudson 1875. *Courtesy of Columbia County Historical Society.*

Hudson 1835. *Courtesy of Hudson Public Library.*

Dedicated to:

Hudson's Seniors,
who are worth listening to,
and
The late Mayor William D. Allen,
whose cheerful honesty
made Hudson a better place.

PREFACE

THE EARNEST YOUNG, WELL, YOUNGISH man approaches the elderly lady on the street. His task is delicate, but he musters all his formidable skills of tact and finesse as he engages her in friendly conversation. "So, Mrs. K.! Tell me all about the whores on Diamond Street!" Her look of genuine horror freezes him into the ground.

He targets another victim. This woman has lived in Hudson for over eight decades. "So, well... uh... Hi! You know, I'm writing a book, and it's, um, well... about the old red light district and the raid and everything, and I was, uh... wondering if you knew anything about it." Referring to the street that shaped the town's image for nearly 200 years, she replies, "What red light district?"

The youngish man relaxes in a coffee shop, tape recorder by his side. He tries once again, putting the delicate question to the owner's mother, who certainly had been a spectator to the era. Her reply? "You put in your book that I said there were a lot of nice kids living here then, and they all got good jobs, and that's all I have to say!" So far he's batting a thousand.

This is a book about people and the mood of an era which ended not so long ago. It is about a little town with a very big, public history of prostitution and a not-so-secret underworld populated by madams, and gangsters, and johns, co-existing with nice, wholesome citizens who went about their business in fiercely blissful ignorance.

There will not be a tremendous number of facts and figures to be found in these pages, not because I couldn't unearth them—in the end the research was done and many different folks spoke up—but because it's not that kind of history. Rather, I want the reader to experience life as it was in Hudson, New York, to see the same ghosts I see when walking around this old place—ladies sweeping through Batchellor's Fancy Goods store wearing gowns with trains and bustles which they used to conceal the items they were shoplifting; Legs Diamond emerging from what is now a burned-out shell on Warren Street after having gotten a shave and a haircut; whores shouting to out-bid each other for the attentions of a customer under the windows of the former public high school; the limp body of a young woman dangling from a scaffold in front of the building where the local newspaper is now printed. When you sit today in a certain stone-walled office in that building, you can almost hear the desperate, whispered prayers that she uttered more than 150 years ago.

The stories and anecdotes, no matter how fictional they may seem, are all true. Most (but not all) of the names used are real. But keep in mind that many madams worked under aliases, changing them so often that even they sometimes lost track of who they were in a given year. Some key players, however, remain unidentified. These are those for whom events described happened within living memory, and if someone was acquitted of a crime, as far as this author is concerned, printing his name does not add to the story. Also, the individuals I could name do not deserve the disproportionate blame (or credit) they would receive for the creation of a system of institutionalized vice which was, after all, carefully passed on from generation to generation.

The information found here was culled from old newspapers, court records, confidential reports to governors, private letters, an unpublished thesis, and most importantly peoples' memories, some pre-dating World War I. Almost everyone who lived in Hudson before 1950 has a story to tell, whether it concerns the activities of a prostitute on the job or the impressions of a young boy delivering ice cream to a naked lady.

Over 65 interviews were conducted with insiders and spectators, and to those people I am forever grateful. Many, if not most, were anxious that their names not be mentioned, but special thanks is owed to historian and professor Dr. Gary Levine for his guidance and for opening his Hudson, New York, Depression Era Collection for use by the author. Mrs. Margaret Schram very graciously shared her research into the "Christmas Murder;" Ms. Marchella Beigel of RSVP made available hours of valuable video-taped interviews with seniors who described growing up in Hudson; Mr. Bruce

Bohnsack showed infinite patience as I combed through his extensive photo collections; and Mr. George Jurgsatis waded through seas of rough drafts, valiantly trying to keep me in line. Patricia H. Davis, Matina Billias, and Mr. Kenelm Burrows corrected my spelling and provided valuable critiques. The staffs of the Columbia County Historical Society, Hudson Public Library, the Columbia-Greene College Library, the State Library at Albany, and the New York Public Library deserve my gratitude. Ms. Angela Turner, formerly of WHUC Radio in Hudson, made my book the subject of her call-in talk show. A certain old-time politician was equally generous with his recollections, giving me hours of pleasure as I listened to him tell of the people and events he has known. When asked to describe the Warren Street of his youth, he didn't bat an eye as he placidly listed in order every business and shopkeeper on the nine-block street from 60 years past. Somewhere in the 300-block he slipped on a man's name. "Oh! My memory is so bad!," he said as he struggled to remember an obscure businessman who died before World War II. I also know now every kind of car he drove from 1923 to 1991. He liked Kaisers.

Others who were generous with childhood memories included Mrs. Estocia Berry, Mrs. Marion Stone, Mr. Mike Cordato, Dr. Harold Levine, Mr. Kenny Propst, Mr. Edward Thompson, Mr. Charlie Beecher, Mr. Clayton Waltermire, and more, too numerous to mention. Mrs. Evelyne West told me of being a schoolteacher during that period. Mrs. Carl Wichmann told of her late husband's perspective in the State Police, and Miss Nathalie Lampman, former editor of the *Daily Star*, provided insights into the press's reaction to various raids and scandals. And then there are dozens of people who, for whatever reasons, wish to remain anonymous—those who would rather keep their associations with a colorful past secret, but who gleefully told me of them anyway. To all these people, thank you, and again thank you.

Finally I must express my deepest gratitude to Ms. Debbie Allen and Ms. Suzanne LaRosa, who had faith enough in my abilities and the value of this story to want to publish it. But then, it's a story that tells itself.

Bruce E. Hall
Hudson, New York

TABLE OF CONTENTS

1: WELCOME TO HUDSON

Hudson, New York, July 4, 1939—
a Norman Rockwell painting in motion.[1]
Eleven thousand people live in this
venerable old town perched on a bluff high above the
Hudson River, where handsome Victorian buildings
create a muted patina of bricks and brownstone. Ten
streets wide and ten streets deep, Hudson is the biggest
town in Columbia County, and home to a courthouse, a
hospital, a rambling old fieldstone orphanage, the
Home for Retired Volunteer Firemen, and its attached
Fire Fighters' Museum, said to be the biggest in the
country. Local people flock to Warren Street to shop at
Sam's Food Market, Richmann's Dress Shop, Berman's
Furniture, and Rogerson's Hardware. There is a Macy's
here, but it is only a small housewares shop. Legend
has it that in the previous century, two brothers named

Macy decided to open dry goods stores. One stayed in Hudson, and the other went to... but then, it's only a legend.

From Franklin Square at the base of the hill, where the waters of the Hudson River lap at the stone foundations of buildings the Dutch left behind when the settlement was still known as Claverack Landing, you can take the car ferry to the little village of Athens, ten minutes across the Hudson. Or you can board a long, sleek, dayliner for New York City, 120 miles and seven hours' sailing time to the south. One way fare: $1.60. Close by is the quaint little train station dwarfed by the giant black steam engines standing ready to sweep you off to New York or Boston, Montreal or Rochester, Chicago, New Orleans, Hollywood.

The City of Hudson is, however, inhabited by a domestic lot. Their pleasures are local ones: picnics in the country; swimming in the River or at nearby Spook Rock; softball, sailing, fishing, or hunting in the woods beyond the orchards and cherry farms that surround the town. Tonight the Polish National Alliance is sponsoring a benefit dance at 1 South Front Street. There will be plenty of Polish sausages and beer, not to mention the Cornhusker's Orchestra. Admission is 25 cents. There is a carnival all week at the rear of the Claverack Fire House, four miles away, with a band concert and "ground gift" every evening. Or if you want to make the trip, you could drive out to Miller's Grill in Red Hook, where they have dancing every Thursday and Saturday to the music of Joe Abbotts and his Five Colored Boys, alleged to be the "Snappiest Band in the County."

The three movie theaters are busy. The grand new Community, with its ornate balcony and row of stately white columns, is featuring "Naughty but Nice" with Zazu Pitts and Ronald Reagan. The city's young people might be more inclined to go off to see "Parents on Trial" at the Star Theater. The 25 cents admission also includes the Three Stooges in "Saved by the Bell," a cartoon, novelty short, sports newsreel, and free dish for the ladies. (If they see enough movies, they can collect a whole set, including matching salt and pepper shakers.) Children can go to the matinee of "Scouts to the Rescue" at the Warren, where they are offering "Free Toys to the Kiddies!" according to the newspaper, but then the Warren has to compete with the Boys' Club, which shows movies to the little ones for a nickel.

For those who don't feel like going out on the warm summer day, the radio offers such diversions as Dick Tracy, Farm Paper of the Air, Associated Glee Clubs of America, Summertime Swing, and The Jell-O Program. On this particular night, however, most people will probably gather down by the River to watch the fireworks, conducted by an expert in pyrotechnics brought all the way from Schenectady for the occasion. The starbursts and glittering rockets reflect in the water, providing twice the show, all for free.

Hudson has 20 churches, six banks, two daily newspapers, and diverse organizations including the American Legion, Veterans of Foreign Wars, Daughters of the American Revolution, Young Men's Christian Association, Jewish Men's Club, Masons, Elks, Moose, Odd Fellows, and Colored Citizens Club, supposedly the only black-owned club between New York and Buffalo.

The banner headline in the *Daily Star* is "Negro Killed in Crash." A local man has been killed in an automobile accident with two others injured. Someone started a small fire when they tossed a firecracker into the waiting room of the Hudson/Athens ferry. Kids acting up again. Elsewhere on the page we read that King George VI of England and Prime Minister Chamberlain are warning the Nazis to lay off Poland. Foreigners acting up again.

Today, most of the city's residents crowd the sidewalks of Warren Street to watch what is proving to be one of the largest Fourth of July parades ever. Clutching their Italian ices and tiny 48-star flags, people cheer and wave as 13 volunteer fire companies, including all six of Hudson's own (six shiny red trucks kept in six spotless Victorian firehouses), march smartly up the cobbled avenue accompanied by marching bands, top-hatted officials, and breathless young boys running alongside. Hudson Mayor William Wortman waves at the crowds from the back of an open black Packard. The Mt. Carmel Boys' Drum and Bugle Corps of Poughkeepsie (30 miles to the south) escorts the Evans Hook and Ladder Company and ends up winning the first prize cup for "musical organizations." The Chatham Fire Department has brought along its beautiful, brand-new ambulance with two male attendants in starched white riding proudly in the front. Little boys are delighted when it roars into life and breaks ranks with sirens wailing and lights flashing, rushing to the aid of the small child who has injured himself when a firecracker blew up in his hand.

Riding a chestnut mare and flanked by two mounted aides, solid and respectable Sheriff Milton V. Saulpaugh, acting as Grand Marshal, surveys the spectators along the parade route the way a medieval lord reviews the peasants on his fief. He holds a hand out in greeting towards the upturned faces of the men in straw boaters and the women in light summer dresses, their bright-eyed, small children dressed in colorful jumpers. The factory workers, merchants, farmers, and professionals are a relatively happy, well-fed lot. A man might earn 18 or even 22 dollars a week at a local factory making pocketbooks or cement, enough to afford a nice twenty-five-dollar-a-month apartment. Saulpaugh seems to know them all: Frank Warner, the watchmaker; Mr. Silverstein, the tailor; Mrs. Redmond, the milliner; Mike Finn, the barber; elegant Mrs. Benson standing on the brownstone stoop of her somewhat forbidding old mansion; and Mr. D'Nofrio, who is so fat his children have to tie his shoes. The Sheriff nods at Dr. Levine and his wife standing in front of their Warren Street home. The young general practitioner charges $1.50 for an office visit and $2.00 for house calls ($3.00 if it's after midnight). Sometimes he's paid with bushels of vegetables or freshly killed chickens. Sometimes he leaves a few dollars behind in households too poor to afford sheets for the half dozen kids packed into the single bed. He has been known to sleep in a farmyard all night in his 1927 Packard waiting for a baby to decide to be born and to dispense "family advice" as readily as medicine.

Suddenly Sheriff Saulpaugh's horse stumbles, hooves slipping on the oily pavement. The crowd gasps as the chestnut mare falls heavily to the ground. But the Sheriff reacts quickly. Jumping clear as the horse goes down, he lands uninjured. Quickly he coaxes the frightened animal to her feet and deftly leaps back into the saddle. Grinning and waving his hat, he has become a portly Lone Ranger.

Families cheer. The parade continues. The whistle from the riverboat to New York sounds in the distance as she approaches the dock at the foot of the hill.

Meanwhile, Paul Cocheran pilots his 1935 Ford V-8 sedan down State Street, trying to find a way over to his barber shop on Fourth. He and his new wife are traveling in from the country and find much of their way blocked by the noisy procession on Warren. Now as he carefully steers around the parked cars and farm wagons of families who also have come in for the excitement, he plans on cutting across Third Street and up Columbia so he can stop and pick up something from the barber shop before going home. Stray children on bicycles and teenagers seeking to escape for a moment the watchful gaze of their parents dart here and there across his path as he slowly makes the turn onto Third and another onto Columbia.

But something is wrong.

Very wrong.

A sight far more startling than a few kids with melting ice cream cones causes him to stop dead in his tracks. His wife, who has been dozing off in the July heat, sits up, suddenly alert, and tries to comprehend the scene before her. She stares and stares, her mouth opening wide in utter disbelief. Mrs. Cocheran addresses her husband. "What *is* all this?" she cries.

The narrow street, parallel to Warren, is lined with small, undistinguished, wooden houses. Two thirds up the block is a lumberyard. Just on the left shine the lights of a small bar. Right down the middle, a lone marching band has somehow separated from the rest of the parade one block to the south and moves slowly along in formation, blaring out a John Philip Sousa tune. And there, hanging out of the windows of all those shabby old houses, are women. Dozens of them. Women of every size and shape, one, sometimes two in every window, leaning out, shouting, gesticulating, vying for the attention of the men marching in the street.

"Hi, gang! Here we are!"

"Come and get it!"

"Hey boys! We've got beautiful girls inside!"

"Wanna make a baby, baby?"

It is an absolute circus with half-naked girls shouting to be heard over the March King's music. A large woman in her thirties, dressed in nothing but a pale blue negligee, cups her ample breasts and makes loud kissing noises with her very red painted lips. A skinny, younger blond stands in an upstairs window and, laughing, opens her robe to reveal everything she has to offer underneath. A pretty young woman dressed in a white satin dressing gown, her dark hair elaborately curled, sits on a ground floor windowsill and beckons to a teenaged horn player who misses his note as he turns, distracted by her beauty. Incongruously, she holds a large, identically dressed baby doll in her lap, with a bright red rosary around its neck. There is a huge fat woman with a little mustache standing in a doorway, who really looks more like a very ugly man in an old housedress and slippers with a pair of black silk stockings rolled down to just below her great, fleshy knees. An attractive, middle-aged lady surveys the scene with a practiced, mercenary eye while a couple of little dogs yap hysterically at her heels. Two girls on the first floor of an unassuming bungalow giggle wildly as they shake their exposed, white bottoms at the street, while the marchers themselves grin like morons and struggle to play, walk, and think about the delights behind those windows all at the same time.

Mrs. Cocheran is new to Hudson. She stares, horrified, at the Bacchanalian scene unfolding in front of her. The lady turns to her husband and demands once again, "Paul! *What* is going on?"

Paul Cocheran can feel his face turning scarlet as he considers his options. Should he tell her it's a big party? A group of escapees from the Girls' Reformatory? An outpouring of patriotic gratitude to a group of visiting firemen from some civic- (and carnally-) minded Hudson matrons? Or should he tell her the truth about Columbia Street, the truth he has known all his life, and how he knows it? Mrs. Cocheran's eyes bore into the side of Paul's head as he embarks on the solution that men have used with their wives since time immemorial: He lies through his teeth.

"I don't know anything about this stuff!" he shouts as he guns the Ford's engine and races around the disintegrating band formation.

Mrs. Cocheran sits in pensive silence, staring out the window. In Hudson, New York in 1939 you can buy six rolls of toilet paper for 19 cents, a steak dinner for $1.00, a man's suit for $15.50, a new Packard for $1,073.00, and a 98-acre farm with a barn and a six-room house for $3,500.00 (25% cash down). You can also get 20 minutes with a prostitute in one of more than a dozen whore houses for $2.00 (not including extras).

Susan Cocheran is the last to know.

2: THE EARLY HISTORY

COLUMBIA STREET, THREE BLOCKS FROM THE River. A 10 minutes' walk will take you out the north end of town. But then, an 11 minutes' walk will take you out the south end of town. It isn't a very big town. This part of Columbia was called Diamond Street until 1926, a name which many people would continue to use for years.

No one can say exactly when they first opened, the brothels, bordellos, bawdy houses, bagnios, houses of ill repute, houses of ill fame, disorderly houses—the whore houses. They had been here so long that people just accepted them as a fact of life. Taking a nocturnal walk down the pokey little street in the shadow of the public high school, you could hear the women's voices whispering, soliciting, summoning you to taboo pleasures. You looked in the direction the murmuring was coming from, but all you could see was the suggestion of a pair of eyes and a female silhouette through the louvers of tightly closed shutters. You went up the walk to take your chances and the madam let you in the back door. In time, you learned who they were and, although they'd never admit it, most Hudson residents knew the sex merchants' names the same way they knew the names of the other merchants in town. The madams of Columbia Street kept their business to their block and knew to keep a low profile—except, of course, when serenaded by a marching band in the middle of a slow workday. In return for this consideration, the citizens of Hudson tacitly agreed to ignore them. The riverboats sailed, the church suppers took place, the parades marched up and down the streets in studied oblivion to the licentious exertions taking place very nearly, but not quite, out of everyone's line of vision. Those respectable Elks, Odd Fellows, Colored Citizens and ladies of the D.A.R. had convinced themselves that there was nothing much out of the ordinary, that every all-American town of 11,000 had one, or maybe two, or perhaps 15 whore houses that attracted every man for 200 miles with two dollars and a sex drive.

The names and faces changed over the years. The titles to the little houses had passed from owner to owner, but their purpose had remained largely the same since the Quakers allowed the first house of ill repute to become established here in the early seafaring days of the community. Probably it was an adjunct to some tavern. Perhaps it involved one of the dozens of slaves living here in those decades. Perhaps an enterprising madam from New York saw a golden business opportunity, and fleeing the ruthless competition in what was known as the "Holy

Ground" (eighteenth-century New York City's most notorious red light district), loaded her "Ladies of Pleasure" onto a river sloop and headed for the not-for-long virgin hunting grounds of Hudson.

The mists in the river valley still hold the whispered legends of women known as the "Jackson Whites." Jackson, they say, was an agent of the British government during the Revolution, assigned the task of providing women to the British troops. For weeks he plied the brothels of London, Bristol, Plymouth, and Liverpool, recruiting ladies for His Majesty's service. When he had trouble meeting his quota, he stole what he couldn't buy, sending his men into the poorer districts to kidnap unsuspecting young women and confine them in his ships. When even then he didn't have enough, he detoured through the Caribbean on his way to New York, visiting the slave markets, buying black women, unwanted servants, field hands—Jackson Blacks.

Over 3,000 women were supposedly delivered by Mr. Jackson to the British army occupying New York. They were herded into temporary housing built for them on the far northern edge of the city, which is now a street so far downtown that most people couldn't find it without a map. There the "harlots flourished brazenly as these dives prospered."[1] Flourished, that is, until the British lost the War and the brazen harlots were driven out of town by the victorious Americans in 1783, the same year some New England Quakers were buying land to build a great new city upriver. They fled north, hundreds of panicked prostitutes hitching rides on boats or making their way on foot along the muddy paths that passed for roads along the banks of the River, pitiful bundles of clothes and other possessions strapped to their backs. Many took up residence with Hessian deserters and runaway slaves in the Ramapo Hills. Others settled in the larger Hudson River towns—Yonkers, Newburgh, Kingston, Poughkeepsie, Albany.

The legends may be true. A group of these women could have arrived in Hudson as the first of a long, tainted line. The Quakers would have tolerated a small number. They were good for business and, as everyone knew, occasional sex with a prostitute would keep a man from cheating on his wife and would protect the virtue of respectable ladies, prostitutes, of course, not entirely counting as people.

The mostly Quaker settlers, known to subsequent generations as the Proprietors, first came to what is now Hudson in 1783, well-to-do seafarers from Nantucket and Martha's Vineyard looking to establish an inland harbor safe from pirates and the British Navy. They didn't merely arrive bag and baggage; they sailed their ships up the Hudson River with all the accouterments of an established community lashed to their decks, including disassembled houses. From the very beginning they planned their city with a view toward creating a major inland port, home to trading ships and a whaling industry. They laid out the straight streets and public squares and within three years the town had grown all the way to Fourth Street. The Dutch burghers of nearby Claverack and Kinderhook mistrusted these English-speakers and tried to hinder the growth of their new commercial center by various devious means. Hudson's city fathers responded by hiring a Dutch-speaking spy[2] who would travel the four miles along the cow path to the county seat at Claverack to find out what those wily Hollanders were up to.

Lots of sailors, merchants, and other travelers passed through Hudson in the early days, and the Quaker fathers were careful to see that they were well provided for. Two years after those first houses were unloaded off the decks of the Proprietors' ships, 18 inns competed for the mostly male transient trade. There were taverns and grog shops where one could spend one's wages on a glass of cheap gin or games of cards or dice. Traveling performers and freak shows solicited money in Market Square. (A small scandal erupted in 1807 when some strangers charged a fee to see a mysterious animal called an "East Indian Nondescript." Hundreds paid to look at the exotic creature, until it was discovered that it was merely a bear with its fur shaved off. Public indignation would have been greater had it not been learned that the strangers, far from making a profit, actually lost 25 cents in the venture.[3] Someone had conned the con men.) Hudson was full of all the pleasures and diversions a mother could warn her seafaring son about, and undoubtedly there were plenty of working girls available to soothe a conned man's ego or show a drunken sailor a good time. The Proprietors wanted to make sure the clientele was happy.

The clientele, arriving by water in those early decades, would have found the docks, fifty feet below the Promenade, crowded with warehouses and piles of cargo waiting to be shipped. Some of the Proprietors built their houses there, but it wasn't long before they would be turned into stores and offices and then built over entirely. It was there that people gathered to watch the Mayor and other dignitaries take the maiden voyage of the new ferry to Loonenburg, which would eventually be called Athens. Powered by horses walking in a giant treadmill which in turn operated a paddle wheel, it was much more efficient than the old sail-driven boat that could take all day to cross the River if the winds were wrong. The crowd roared as the new-fangled contraption went out of control and rammed another boat, putting a dent in more than just the festivities. At least the mayor and city council got a good thrill.

Front Street, lined with its brick stores and shipping offices, was the commercial center, wooden sidewalks protecting pedestrians' shoes from the mud and piles of horse manure rotting in the street. Occasionally one would have to shoo away pigs rooting around in the garbage, swine being employed by the Proprietors as municipal sanitation engineers, and gentlemen carried whisks to chase away the battalions of flies that swarmed over everything. Front Street was busy with heavy freight wagons drawn by sturdy teams of horses or oxen headed in and out of Partition Street and the road through Claverack to Massachusetts. Some days there were so many wagons or sleighs with cargo that all the city streets were completely clogged. Quaker gridlock. At the top of Front was Market Square, where stood a large, open-sided building used by farmers to sell their produce, and here was one of the public pumps. Behind it, Parade Hill (eventually to be known as the Promenade), with its beautiful view of the River, provided the rich or the merely pretentious a place to walk in public and show off their finery.

Main Street, which would someday bear the name of Warren, started at Market Square and ran along the crest of the hill at right angles to Front. This was where the "quality" lived. Elegant brick mansions lined the broad avenue. Chestnut trees were still too young to shade the columned porticoes of the spacious new houses. Some sported cupolas on their wood-shingled roofs and many had impressive front doors flanked by whitewashed pilasters or delicately mullioned windows. Everyone had an iron scraper embedded in his marble stoop for removing the inches of muck from the bottoms of his boots before walking on the freshly swept and sanded floors inside. In front of many houses was an iron hitching post and a stone mounting block to assist in making the high step up into a carriage. Pigs and goats roamed this neighborhood as well, joined by the occasional cow escaped from someone's backyard shed. One leading citizen was fined for letting his cow eat up a neighbor's vegetable garden. Sometimes the chickens would get out, too. Such were the travails of living in a city with over 4,000 people, New York's third largest.

One continued up Main Street until one could plainly see the deep gully crossing the road ahead, near the edge of town. So, turning left on Third, one continued over to Diamond. This is where the oil and candle works stood alongside the slaughterhouse. As if the smell of horse dung and rotten garbage wasn't enough, the addition of cattle carcasses and whale blubber caused the area to reek almost beyond tolerance. No one could stand the smell for long and no one really lived out there. The Proprietors chose this place to erect the first school. It was also deemed the perfect spot for illicit love.[4]

It is perverse poetry of the most exquisitely sublime nature that caused Hudson's first bawdy houses to share a street with a sperm oil works, but there it is. Exactly how many brothels there were is unknown. Probably there were several, small and cheaply built, hardly more than two- or three-roomed cabins, heated by open fireplaces, lit by little oil lamps or rushes dipped in grease. At night, groups of drunken sailors and wagon drivers would stagger up the streets, which during one part of the month were dimly lit by whale oil lamps set on poles, or by the moon during the other part. Ever mindful of saving a penny, the Proprietors decreed that if the moon was more than half full, no street lamps would be lit. It didn't matter if clouds or rain obscured the moonlight, or that Hudson whalers brought in sperm oil by the ton. If the almanac said the moon was out, the lamps went unlit, the oil unburned. Of course, on dark nights the sailors could find the houses by the smell.

Not that the women smelled very good either, but then nobody did. Body lice was the norm, and bathing was not only considered unhealthy, it was extremely difficult in an era when all the water had to be carried by hand from one of the public pumps and heated over a wood fire. Hudson had some wooden water pipes, but it would be a long time before Diamond Street saw any indoor plumbing. People usually bathed their faces and hands, and perhaps the women found a way to clean a little more, but why should they? Even the magnificent Napoleon, around 1800, sent the following message to his beautiful Josephine: "Will be home in three weeks. Don't wash."[5]

As for the ladies' backgrounds, the patterns never really changed through the years. Single women had very few ways to earn money, and poverty has always forced people to extremes. Some of the girls probably came from remote farms, seeking escape from an oppressive father, an abusive husband, a life of mind-numbing tedium. Some were hardened women from New York or Albany, and some were addicted to gin, the drug of choice among the poor. Some of the girls were young. Perhaps very young. Since it was common knowledge that sex with a virgin would cure a man of venereal disease, enterprising madams would charge double as they passed off their juvenile workers as undefiled to a constantly changing clientele. It is not clear how the women would get cured. People were not too shocked. In New York State the legal age of sexual consent was all of 10—10 years of age until the very last decade of the nineteenth century.[6] Male lawmakers of the new state were just expressing their ideas about the female's role in society.

For years the Quakers tolerated this "necessary evil" of prostitution. Sometimes there were problems. There would be drunken fights, beatings, petty thievery. Occasionally a prostitute or her boyfriend would cause trouble, but they could be disciplined and sent away. There were stocks and a whipping post, and undesirables were sometimes run out of town in an elaborate ceremony that involved leading the malefactor by a rope through the streets, pausing at each corner, having his offenses read by the town crier to the accompaniment of drums, and then whipping the daylights out of him until the party got to the border of the town. Such punishment was reserved for drunks and chronic troublemakers, and presumably the person would hike up to Claverack to lick his or her wounds. Literally.

One of the first things the Proprietors did was to build a jail on Front Street between Main and Diamond, at the head of the alley which would thenceforth be known by the name of "Prison Alley." This structure, sturdily constructed of logs with iron grates over its little windows, was considered more than sufficient to hold the anticipated drunks and felons. Sufficient, that is, until the first prisoner incarcerated there used a large augur secreted under his clothes to bore his way through the wall and escape. In 1800 a new, brick jail was built on the corner of Main and Fourth. This building became one of the boundaries to the little square that saw Hudson's two public executions. One of them, the hanging of Miss Peggy Dinsmore in 1817 for the murder of a child, was attended by half the county. It was only later that they discovered they had hung the wrong person. Ooops. As for the prostitutes, however, as long as they stayed in their own neighborhood and didn't bother anybody, no one minded much. After all, people came for miles to see them and that brought money into the city. This same sentiment would be echoed for nearly two centuries.

Early financial reverses and outright economic depressions stymied Hudson's growth and helped the sex trade. President Jefferson's Embargo Act of 1807 almost ruined the shipping industry. The War of 1812 didn't help much either. The whaling business succumbed to competition, and eventually the discovery of petroleum in Pennsylvania eliminated the market for sperm oil altogether. During the depression of 1837, all the land surrounding the city was sold for the formation of a new town called Greenport, leaving Hudson stranded on exactly 2.5 square miles of ground. Her only outlet was the River, but soon the railroad came through and they chose to lay the line on causeways built directly across the mouths of Hudson's two little harbors, cutting them off forever. Gone was room for expansion, gone were Hudson's farms and orchards, gone was the source for her water supply, gone was the shipping that had been the very reason for her existence. Hudson's new generation of merchants didn't think of any of that. They just looked towards the cash dangling in front of their noses and closed their eyes. They still didn't light the streets or build proper schools. But they could sure smell the money from those famous houses of ill fame.[7]

By the 1840s, the bawdy houses were no longer on the edge of town. Hudson had grown around them. Even though the shipping industry was in decline, the population had grown to nearly 7,000, and the streets beyond Fourth were filling with their homes. People began to complain to the City Council about the "riotous gatherings"[8] on Diamond Street. The rowdies and drunks who patronized the saloons and gambling dens on Front Street would make their noisy way past the mansions on Warren as they sought some late night action with the Diamond Street ladies.

In the summer of 1843, Hudson's respectable citizenry was riveted by news of one Mrs. Betsey Smith who was, according to the *Columbia County Washingtonian*, a "modern Jezebel," importing her 14-year-old niece from the country to work in her "house of *some* sort of fame." The girl had been jailed on a charge of vagrancy, and was suffering the further punishment of repeated visits from the zealous ladies of the Martha Washington temperance society, who not only attempted to improve her morals, but "obtained from her a 'long list of names' of young, (not all young) men, who have visited her during her brief career of frailty." In a grand display of "boiling indignation," the *Washingtonian* promised to publish the list so that the men could be "held up to the gaze and scorn of the world." Even though they didn't make good on their threat, the newspaper's office received a steady stream of panicky male visitors, anxious to safeguard their heretofore good reputations.[9]

Hudson's Common Council, meeting a few days later, grumbled about the bad element drawn by "the numerous houses of ill fame with which our city is disgraced,"[10] but they really couldn't do much about it. There was no true police force, only a nearly powerless (and frequently drunk) collection of "constables," and in order for an arrest to be made, a complaint had to be sworn under oath. Usually that involved some upstanding citizen admitting publicly that he had actually been inside a brothel, which would have made him a good deal less upstanding. The teenaged prostitute was eventually sentenced to 30 days on a vagrancy charge, and Mrs. Smith was jailed in lieu of $500 bond while the authorities tried to decide what to do with her. No record remains of what their final judgment was.

In 1844 the county population rebelled against the last, great feudal landowners in America and embarked upon what history would call the Anti-Rent Wars. Hudson was the center of activity, and hundreds of troops were stationed here for months for the purpose of maintaining order. Nothing breeds prostitution more than a captive military audience, and the Hudson harlots had a field day. Despite, or perhaps because of, the declining economy around them, vice in Hudson had become a self-perpetuating industry. The midnight activities of Diamond Street had grown into an institution known up and down the river.

"Colorful" is one way to describe some of the characters hanging out on Diamond Street in the 1860s and 70s. The little knoll on Front at the foot of Diamond was known as "Vinegar Hill," and on a warm summer evening "disorderly women" could be found loitering there, looking for some sport. Neighbors complained and police constables were constantly being called to keep the peace. One August night in 1869, Maggie Garity and Ann Murphy, "a healthy pair of damsels," came into town for "a bit of fun, to the detriment of the neighborhood."[11] They were fined for disturbing the peace. "Big Bridget" was a chronic troublemaker. Once, after having received a complaint, a police constable found her passed out under a cart. She spent a few days in jail. Loose women were frequently reported to be fighting in the street, but the constables were rarely quick enough to catch them at it. For more predictable vice, one needed to visit one of the established brothels further up the block.

George and Kate Best had the place at number 165 Diamond.[12] From the outside it appeared to be a cute little cottage, with a bay window and gingerbread brackets on the eaves. Inside, George would sell you a glass of beer or tell you a dirty story while Kate would introduce you to one of her zoftig beauties. She would have as few as two or as many as nine, depending on whether or not the circuit court had filled the town with visiting law clerks and plaintiffs looking for a good time. Mrs. Best would swirl around the little parlor in her huge hoop skirt, while the girls would pose seductively, dressed in loose wrappers, providing a tantalizing glimpse of corset, garter, and flesh underneath. Lots of flesh. It was reported that one popular young woman who had been ill was, with the restoration of her health, beautiful once again, as she had "gained seventy-five pounds." In Hudson, you always got a lot for your money.

Although there had been an ordinance on the books since 1859 outlawing bawdy houses and gambling parlors, by looking at the arrest records one would never know it. George Best's behavior, however, made it possible for his wife to be cited three times in one year. The afternoon of July 19, 1869 was a typically quiet Sunday until George and four of his friends decided to pay a call at the Central House Hotel, at the corner of Warren and Fifth. The five had been drinking since the day before and although no one was exactly sure of their motives, they reeled into the lobby and started picking fights. Someone was soon sent running to find a constable, and in due time Officer Duffy arrived on the scene. The drunks, who were having a wonderful time, beat him up and threw him into the muddy street before continuing with their melee. Not one to be dismissed so easily, Officer Duffy went and got a gun. Returning to the Central House, he started shouting threats from the sidewalk, attracting a post-church crowd of some 200 people to watch the excitement. George and his teenaged friend Johnny drew their guns and started firing. The crowd of church-goers went diving for cover. A spirited gunfight ensued between Duffy and the two men in the hotel, during which nobody, amazingly, was hit, although a bullet did just miss a lady sitting in the window of Mrs. Lay's house and lodged "in a box of goods upon a shelf." George Best and his crony Johnny escaped, but the citizens of Hudson rushed into the hotel to hold the other three (unarmed) men until they could be properly arrested. The crowd, now a mob, soon were seeking justice on the ringleader, George Best. Hordes of people descended on the little brothel on Diamond Street with Officer Duffy in the lead, but were disappointed to find that the gunmen were already in flight towards the river. Duffy and the throng surged after the two, and reached the water just in time to see them escaping, George by row boat, Johnny by running north along the railroad tracks. Somehow, Police Constable Duffy, with a gun and dozens of angry men to assist him, had managed to let the two ruffians slip through his fingers. He was not having a good day.

Summoning Officers Gifford and Nye, Duffy decided to take out his frustrations on Kate Best and her girls at number 165. The mob turned around and headed back up Diamond Street, but found that two of Kate's "soiled doves" had also taken flight, sensing trouble. While Kate and one girl were taken to the police court, the crowd pursued the other two women until at last, all four were facing the judge. Ida Vail was released. Mollie Wright was run out of town. And for some reason, the woman who gave her name as Nellie Saucy (popularly known thereafter as "Saucy Nellie") was handed a stiff fine and six months at hard labor. Telling the court "you've been damned hard on me," her judgement was thrown out on appeal. As the madam, Mrs. Best received the maximum sentence the Hudson ordinances allowed: She was fined $25.[13]

George Best became something of an obsession for Officer Duffy. For months he sought the fugitive, lying in wait night after night in the alley behind the Bests' house, and spending part of his own meager salary in an attempt to hunt the man down. Several times there were rumors that George had come back to town. Once, Duffy actually saw him, but the hooligan and his friends turned and ran, quickly outdistancing the police constable. Twice more, a neighbor swore out complaints, enabling Duffy to harass his nemesis by running in Mrs. Best and Saucy Nellie. Twice more Kate paid their fines. At long last, as winter descended on the little town, George resurfaced and was arrested. In great triumph, Police Constable Duffy saw Mr. Best go before the judge. He was convicted of a misdemeanor and served a short time in jail. Duffy quit his job and went to work for the railroad. George's long-suffering wife died in 1876 and, never one to dwell on appearances, he waited a month and married one of his dead wife's employees. He was then 45 years old. George and his new wife moved next door to number 163, and Kate's old business was taken over by another couple. The late Kate Best probably had the better end of the deal.

George Best had been in trouble with the law since he was six years old. Years after the "Sunday Riot," he admitted in court, where he was testifying as a character witness (if that can be believed), that he had been arrested for three "petty crimes" in the previous decade.

"Weren't you indicted for shooting a man?" demanded the judge.

"Oh yes!" he replied with a gap-toothed grin. "That makes four!" His victim later admitted that he had deserved to be shot. The gun fight on Warren Street wasn't even mentioned.[14]

It was John Conroy's character that Mr. Best was trying to defend in court, which is an indication of what sort of person he was. Conroy, a brothel owner in nearby Kingston, was married to a popular prostitute named Ada. Young and beautiful, she was always corseted and bustled in the latest fashion. For some reason, Ada was devoted to Conroy, even when a local "upstanding citizen" complained about his business activities and Conroy tried to get even by blowing up him and his family by filling the cellar of their house with gunpowder. The victims survived, but when Conroy was sentenced to life in prison at hard labor, Ada announced to the world that she wouldn't live without him and that she had taken poison. The community anxiously waited for her to die, but languish as she might, she didn't so much as lose her appetite: the next time Ada appeared in public, she had a new dress, a new boyfriend, and seemingly not a care in the world. She also had a new "shop" in Hudson.

Up the street from the Best establishment lived James Weeks and his girlfriend Mary Brace, known to the world as "Nell Weeks." James and Nell kept some working girls, eventually hiring Saucy Nellie after she had left the Bests' employ. Things went fine until Nellie fell in with a low-life sleaze named Eddie Shultz. Together they robbed the brothel of $200 and some of Nell Week's jewelry, taking off cross-country. Nell was furious with Nellie and sent a detective after them. Laboriously he tracked the two by train, going from country depot to country depot, finally catching up with them in a Connecticut boardinghouse, living as a married couple. Even though they had nothing much to show for it, Eddie and Saucy Nellie had spent much of the money. However, Nell Weeks got her jewelry back and the thieves were returned to Hudson in irons to be thrown into jail, much to the amusement of the townspeople who had followed the case with relish.

One of Phoeba Flagg's girls solved the shopping problem by using the enormous bustle under her skirt as a shoplifting aid. It was amazing what one could conceal under a four-foot train. Sometimes unsuspecting men, struggling to keep up with women's fashions, would tread on her hem when she was in a crowded store and the lady would imperiously turn to stare the poor saps into the ground. Lucky for her, bustles stayed in style for years.

"Hat" Benton lived in a tiny house on Prison Alley wedged in between Diamond and Warren. She was one of Hudson's few black madams and although her girls, Annie and Belle, were black also, most of her customers were white. Visitors to Hat's place always had to remember that if they crossed her, they had to suffer a torrent of withering obscenities from her mother, Jane. The old lady was legend. Belle used some pretty strong language too, but only when she was falling-down drunk, which was usually.

Beautiful Cora Young presented a pitiful picture when she was on trial for murder. The girl was remorseful in the extreme and exhibited a strong desire to mend her wicked ways. The all-male jury was quick to acquit her, and the family of one them, Martinder E. Durkee, took a special interest in the young woman. Mrs. Durkee even went so far as to issue Cora a public invitation to move into the Durkee household in an attempt to reform her. The girl accepted and proved very receptive to the familial love she found there. Cora eloped with Mr. Durkee that December.

Eliza Traver had not worked as a prostitute for long. At the age of 37, it wasn't so easy for her, but her husband, Jerome, had left her and in pre-welfare America, she was desperate to support herself. Not able to find a job, and not willing to move to the Alms House, she set up in business alone. Soon she was visited by the bane of the prostitutes' existence. Eliza found she was pregnant. Without the resources to support a child, she turned to Abby Cable, who, the other girls told her, was the best abortionist around. Mrs. Traver's body was discovered on a blood-soaked mattress, the wounds from her operation infected and putrid. Miss Cable was nowhere to be found.

And then there was John V. Kiere.

3: A Christmas Murder

UDSON, NEW YORK, DECEMBER 20, 1876—a Currier and Ives painting in motion.[1] The little city sparkles under a mantle of freshly fallen snow. There is a slight sting in the air from the wisps of low-hanging smoke from fires in hundreds of grates and parlour stoves, while the streets are full of sleighs pulled by smartly trotting teams, the bells on their harnesses filling the ears with a cheerful, Christmas jangling. Frank Nelson's horse is spooked by something at the corner of Third and Warren and bolts up the street, broadsiding a sleigh driven by Albert Downing. Mr. Downing is thrown into a snow bank, but not injured before the animal can be stopped. Citizens, bundled up against the cold, trudge the sidewalks of Warren Street, buying Christmas presents and admiring the festive window displays. Christmas trees, their boughs dripping with acorns, strings of berries, ornaments of blown glass, and tiny wax tapers attached to the ends of branches, appear in churches and the parlours and drawing rooms of Hudson's more prosperous residents. They stand waiting for Christmas Eve when, with all their candles lit and branches hung with beautifully wrapped treasures, they will be surrounded by elegantly dressed children and ladies and gentlemen, holding hands and singing carols, accompanied by a couple of maids holding buckets of water in case the candles get out of hand.

Civic-minded residents have a variety of complaints to register this season, however. A man walks into the police station claiming that he has been accidentally shot in the head by hunters on the outskirts of town. The police chief sends him to a doctor and issues a request to people to please be more careful in the future. Goats still roam freely, as well as swarms of poor children from the neighborhood north of Warren, standing on street corners, begging money from the more well-heeled Christmas shoppers. A proposal is made to close the "colored school" because only seven or eight children attend. It's not that Hudson's black families don't want their children to be educated, they just prefer to send them to the "white" schools instead.[2]

Meanwhile, in a little house on Diamond Street between Fourth and Fifth, Mrs. Robert Giles Spaulding hurriedly packs a large carpet bag. Her bedroom is cold as she folds her one silk dress, the brown one with tasseled fringe and draperies that she got married in nine months before. Lately she has been trying to save money on coal and just keeps a fire going in the kitchen range downstairs, but that is where her husband sits, sullen and bleary-eyed, and she doesn't want to face him. They seem to fight all the time now, and she has had enough.

At first he was fun, lively and attentive, but then the money started to dry up and he started to drink more. She tried to keep his house clean, to cook food he liked and mend his clothes, but it was hard on what he made. Besides, as soon as he'd earn a dollar he'd spend it on drink in Peeper's Saloon with those loud friends of his. More and more often he'd stagger home drunk after midnight and yell at her because his supper wasn't hot or because the house was cold or because he suspected that she had been entertaining some "gentleman friend." And then there had been the times he hit her. The mornings afterward he'd be all sweetness and apologies and sometimes he'd buy her a little present, but it would soon start all over again. She has wanted to leave for some time, but knew that if she moved in with her mother, Giles would just go and bring her home.

Annie Spaulding fixes her hat in the mirror. She knows that men find her attractive. On occasion, when she has had to walk through Central Square on the way to the market, she has noticed them looking at her large figure. She is not fat, exactly, but she laces her corset tight, emphasizing her curves and giving her a decidedly voluptuous air. Irene Brancari says that she will be a big success and perhaps earn enough money to leave Hudson and Giles behind forever. Annie dreams of a glamorous life in Albany or New York as she shoves in the last of her stockings and struggles to shut the old carpet bag. She throws a dark cloak over her wool dress, and with her peaked bonnet and huge bustle she looks something like a giant goose with a blanket draped over its back, a typical, respectable matron.

As the wife comes down the stairs, the husband can be heard muttering in the kitchen, too drunk to get out of his chair, his empty beer bucket rolling around at his feet. Let him stay there, she thinks. The woman takes one last look at the cheap rented house and its shabby, old furniture and plunges through the door into the cold, afternoon air outside. The carpet bag is heavy, but she marches determinedly down Diamond Street, turns the corner onto Second, and knocks at the portal of the old brick house next to Larry Mack's Saloon. The door is flung open by a woman with a heavily painted face, her hair crimped and curled, her low-cut gown revealing an impressive bosom supported by bone and steel. Mrs. Spaulding looks at her for a moment and says simply, "I'm here, Irene." Irene Brancari smiles, admits her into the whore house, and shuts the door against the cold. Mrs. Spaulding has found refuge. Mrs. Spaulding is 15 years old. [3]

Irene actually lives next door, but this week she is holding down the fort for the real madam of this establishment, her sister, Ellanora Kiere and Ellanora's husband, Johnny. Twenty six-year-old John V. Kiere has taken Ellanora down to New York City for a few days to do some shopping and see some friends. John Kiere is well known in Hudson. Seven years earlier, he was the teenager who joined George Best in the famous drunken shoot-out on Warren Street with the hapless Constable Duffy. Although Johnny had initially escaped by running up the railroad tracks, he soon returned to Hudson where he was apprehended, convicted of disturbing the peace, and sent to prison for a few months. Since that time, he has grown a mustache and become the owner of a saloon at 30 South Front Street and his wife's brothel at 14 North Second. Always a little short-tempered, Johnny has continued to find trouble and has shot five men in his lifetime. Even though only two of them died, all of them deserved it as they had insulted his honor. However, the judge didn't see it that way, and Johnny has had to serve time in prison. In fact, even though he's only been free for a few months, the law still won't leave him alone. He is now out on bail, awaiting trial for assaulting a policeman in Troy. Of course, he swears he didn't do it.

Ellanora Kiere, also 26, dotes on her husband. He set her up in business, taking her out of that low dive she had been working in before, and she owes him everything. Sometimes he can be difficult, especially when he thinks other men are paying too much attention to her, but she has learned to pacify him. Johnny always buys her beautiful things and sees that she is dressed in the latest fashions; however, her beauty is marred by a nasty scar that runs across her face. Ellanora staunchly denies that her husband caused it by beating her. Of course, he did throw a spittoon at her last month in the saloon, but it was her fault as she had gotten him mad. She also denies that he killed their baby in a rage over its crying last summer. It was born dead, she says, while others hold their tongues and look away. At any rate, they have a healthy four-year-old daughter, currently staying with her grandmother, and Ellanora is pregnant again. She looks forward to seeing her children grow up, if they can avoid the consumption and brain fever that seem to cause so many in this neighborhood to die young. [4] Ellanora says she is very happy. As a matter of fact, she insists.

Irene, 19,[5] often helps out at her sister's place. Her husband, Andrew, a "segar" maker, is an affable drunk who wouldn't know $5.00 if it choked him, and fancy ladies can make a lot of money. Working with her is Josephine Maude Clayton, a tough-talking, cigar-smoking woman in her early twenties from Montreal, who has been working as a prostitute for about five years. Although she is of thoroughly English stock, she speaks some French and likes to whisper Gallic nothings into the ears of her customers, making them think they are getting something more rare and mysterious than they really are. They call her "French Maude" and she does very well. Mrs. Hanley also comes down from her place up the block, lending her rather domestic charms to this popular house of ill fame. Annie Spaulding is made to feel welcome, and for the first time in nearly a year she can relax freely with other females without the fear of her husband bursting in, in a jealous rage.

The room is cold and dark when Giles finally wakes up. He has a headache and is stiff from sleeping in the chair for so long. The fire has gone out and no lamps are lit. Fumbling around in the dark, he calls for Annie. Carefully, for his hands are still a little shaky, he strikes the match on the cold stove and raises the chimney of the kerosene lamp on the table. As the white light fills the center of the room, he suddenly remembers the heated argument he had with his wife that afternoon. A vague image of her cloaked figure and a carpet bag enters his mind. Giles steps out into the hall and shouts Annie's name as loudly as he can. There is no answer.

Saturday, December 23, 1876. At about six o'clock, after tea and a light supper, Charles Hermance and his

wife go out shopping for toys for their seven-year-old son.
They find what they want at Mr. Batchellor's store on
Warren below Third. He has reduced prices and stayed
open late to attract last-minute Christmas shoppers. At six-
thirty or seven o'clock, the Hermances part company, she
returning home, he heading for the Saturday night crowd
hanging out in Central Square. It is their long-standing
evening ritual, and Mrs. Hermance quietly accepts her
wifely role without complaint.

As he passes the door of Peeper's Saloon, Charley can
hear the voice of Fidel Wise, telling one of his funny
stories, keeping the men at the bar roaring with laughter.
The twenty-seven-year-old is always ready with a joke or a
song, travelling the state playing the banjo with Carter &
Curry, the almost-famous minstrel troupe. When in
Hudson he sometimes lives with his brother on Front, but
more often shares bed and board with a pretty black
woman he knows from Diamond Street. People talk, but he
doesn't much care. On this particular Saturday he has
spent all afternoon at Peeper's as usual, and cheerfully
waits for good times to find him there.

Giles Spaulding pushes back his chair after finishing a
plate of pork and beans at his aunt's house on State Street,
where he has been living since Annie left him. Silently he
grabs his overcoat and saunters out the door and down
towards Central Square to see if any of his friends are
loafing there. This has generally been his daily routine, but
today he is in a particularly sullen mood since overhearing
that his wife has taken up with that scoundrel, Johnny
Kiere. His ears burn with shame as he recalls the
sniggering comments muttered when those fellows
thought he was out of earshot. Angrily, he offered to

defend his name, but the men just laughed at him and told him to go home to his mama. He digs his hands deeper into his pockets and marches on. Annie. Ordinarily he would just go down to that filthy place and order her to come home with him, like when she tried to move back with her mother last fall, but this is different. The smooth-faced 20-year-old boy isn't sure he wants to tangle with the larger, gun-toting man with the black mustache and the blacker reputation. His ire increases as he realizes his helplessness. The taunts of the other men ring in his ears again. His woman is making a fool of him and she must be taught a lesson.

Down at Central Square, Giles finds the usual crowd, perhaps a little thinner because of the cold. Charley Hermance and his brother hail him from their position under a lamp post, unlit tonight because the moon is out. Giles is glad to have someone with whom to share his frustrations, and soon the little group decides to nurse their troubles over a beer at Mrs. Ricker's Saloon at the corner of Fourth and Prison Alley. They move around the corner to Peeper's Saloon where they take up with Fidel Wise, to drink and talk about Annie and drink some more. They move to Wolf's up the street where they drink and talk of a man's honor and continue drinking. Then they return to Peeper's again. For some reason, Giles and Charley are having trouble walking upright, but they're feeling fearlessly righteous. Somewhere along the line, Giles runs or falls into Harvey Scott, who lets drop the intriguing piece of information that John V. Kiere and wife are known to be in New York City. They have been there all week, and the Kiere bordello is populated only by women. The

Citadel is left unguarded. A dim plan of action starts to form in Giles Spaulding's mushy brain.

Pulling Charley Hermance out onto the sidewalk, he asks for his company to "go see that woman of mine." Charley agrees with woozy enthusiasm, and as they start down the street, Fidel Wise pokes his head out to ask where they are going. "To Kiere's," comes the answer, and Fidel falls in step, always ready to visit another saloon. As they pass the corner of Second Street, Giles and Charley turn right, headed for the small brick brothel 200 feet away. For the first time that evening, Fidel's cheerfulness stumbles. He had thought the party was headed for Johnny Kiere's Saloon on Front Street for another round of drinks and songs, but now he sees his drunken companions' true intent and immediately senses danger. He tries to dissuade them, to encourage them to go back to Peeper's or anywhere else, but Giles taunts him with the name of coward while Charley stares at him with puffy eyes. Fidel relents and reluctantly trots behind as they stumble up the street. Someone has to keep these two out of trouble.

Irene, Annie and Frank Morrison have just put away their wraps after returning from Kiere's Saloon. It has been unusually slow for a Saturday night, but then business always lags around Christmas. Annie has been feeling a little low as she has come to realize that she would be spending the holiday in a whore house, and Irene thought it might be good for her to get out for awhile. Besides, she wanted to show off their new, teenaged attraction to a group of potential clients. Leaving French Maude and Mrs. Hanley behind, the two women socialized with the fellows on Front Street for an hour or two, accompanied by Frank, for it is improper for ladies, even fancy ones, to go into a public place without an escort. Frank performs this service frequently. The young man lives further up Diamond Street with his mother, and likes to hang around the girls at Mrs. Kiere's, doing odd jobs and running errands. Sometimes they give him free samples in return for his services, which keeps him happy and out of the way.

Annie, wearing her silk dress laced so tight she could hardly breathe, smiled and laughed and tried to be agreeable to the men admiring her skin and shape, but her heart wasn't in it. Some of these men knew her family. Some of them had known her since she was a little girl, and there was always the danger that Giles or one of his friends would walk in at any time. She hasn't really minded her work thus far, although she had been nervous at first. It isn't especially difficult, and the money is good. At a dollar per customer, she has already saved more than twice what Giles makes in his best weeks.[6] Still, she was glad when Irene called it a night and they headed for home.

It's about ten o'clock and everyone but Mrs. Hanley is in the kitchen sitting around the stove, talking quietly. The ladies have loosened their stays and shed their dresses in favor of more comfortable woolen wrappers. A light knocking on the front door disturbs them, and French Maude wearily gets up to let in the late night clientele. Frank Morrison is quicker, however, and darts into the bedroom so he can see who it is through the window. Maude is almost to the door when she hears him, calling out in a hoarse, urgent whisper. "It's Spaulding!" he says.

The woman freezes in her tracks. Behind her she can hear Annie's gasp and the creak of a chair as Irene rises to her feet. Spaulding is trouble, Maude knows, but she has handled troublesome men before. The knocking continues, and she can hear the garbled voices of more than one man on the stoop as she steps quickly to the door.

"Who is it?," she asks in her most vulnerable, feminine voice.

"A friend," comes the reply in a slightly menacing tone.

"It's late and I'm all alone here," she says. "Come back another time."

There is a confused pause before Spaulding once again asks to be admitted. Maude once again tells him to go home. This time, however, there is an explosion of profanity from the other side of the door.

"Let me in! I have a right in there! Let me in so I can get that bitch of mine out! That bitch is mine, I tell you! She belongs with me!" Two pairs of fists and boots start pounding and kicking, shattering the peace of the night and causing the women to scream. Maude is sure they'll be in the house in a minute, but the old door holds. "Let me in! If you don't open this door I'll break it down and murder that goddamn bitch of mine and that damned black-mustached fellow too! Goddamnit, let me in!"

The household is in an uproar. Annie stands in the middle of the kitchen, dissolved in tears, clasping and unclasping her hands. French Maude, truly frightened, backs away from the door and almost collides with Irene, who rushes into the hall and pushes past Frank, standing dumbfounded in the threshold of the bedroom. Feeling under the mattress in the dark, she grabs hold of Johnny

Kiere's revolver, kept for just such an emergency. From the kitchen, she can hear Annie wailing hysterically, "Don't let him in! He'll kill me! He'll kill me!"

The pounding continues as Irene, brandishing the weapon, frantically motions Maude back to her previous position at the front of the hallway.

"If you don't get away from that door, I'll shoot!" Maude shouts, trying to keep the trembling out of her voice.

A blood-curdling howl goes up from the stoop outside, and the door is attacked with a new, deadly ferocity. The air is full of the sounds of thunder and cursing, splintering wood and breaking glass as the women, dropping all pretense of bravado, scream together in terror and stampede for the stairway and imagined safety of the second floor, with big, dumb Frank Morrison in the lead.

Mrs. Hanley has remained upstairs throughout the siege, but now wants to take the gun and fire it out the window to frighten the men away. Irene doesn't think that's a good idea, and places the pistol on a chair at the top of the stairs as she tries to figure out what to do. The kicking and profanity go on for one minute, two, three. At this rate it is inevitable that they'll get in eventually. She looks at Annie, an hour ago a sophisticated courtesan, now a badly frightened little girl. Maude has spirit, but she's not so sure about Mrs. Hanley, and as for Frank.... Irene wonders if she can get them out the back and over the high fence, and even if they escape, where would they go? The saloon? The police? She picks up the gun, not sure if she would be able to use it, when suddenly, the pounding stops. The women catch their breath as they wait for the onslaught to continue, but there isn't a sound. Cautiously, Irene creeps to the window, and careful not to show any light, lifts the shade. The stoop is empty. The street is quiet. She decides to send Frank to find a policeman.

Fidel Wise has finally gotten his two friends off the bordello steps and into Larry Mack's saloon next door. He had heard a woman's voice threaten to shoot and felt that discretion would be the better part of valour. For their part, Giles and Charley had been distinctly surprised when the unknown female inside didn't open up to them, and had attacked the door in a paroxysm of offended pride, only to run out of steam and stand, confused, as their display of masculine strength failed to impress the objects of their aggression. There are only a few other customers in Larry Mack's at this late hour, and Fidel hopes that time and a couple of beers will convince Charley and Giles to go home. Anxiously he watches the door, fearful of seeing Johnny Kiere's black moustaches before the trio can make their escape. Telling the others to stay where they are, Fidel steps into the alley to see if it's safe to go.

Johnny and Ellanora Kiere leave their saloon on South Front and start towards the bordello three blocks away. It has been a long trip and Ellanora is tired. They should have been home sooner, but Johnny wanted to get off the train to visit his friends at Sing Sing Prison and again at Poughkeepsie. Their arrival at Hudson's new train station didn't occur until after ten, and then there was no one to meet them, as they were expected hours earlier. At the saloon, they pick up Johnny's bartender, Ed Noonan, and 18-year-old James Carrol, a swaggering punk who had assisted Johnny in assaulting the Troy policeman, just as

Johnny had assisted George Best all those years before. They are to follow along and carry the luggage. As they pass Mary Mackey's brothel on the corner of Union, Ellanora looks up and sees the windows dark and silent. It is a very quiet night. They turn up Warren Street, lit only by the moon and occasional gaslight shining from a window, crunching through the snow past the facades of the big, brick houses. Johnny extends a friendly greeting to a man Ellanora recognizes as Fidel Wise who, for some reason, seems startled and takes off down First Street towards the alley. Just before reaching Second, Sod Kelly rushes up to Johnny and breathlessly informs him that "someone is raising hell, trying to get in" to his wife's whore house around the corner. Johnny and James Carrol break into a run, but Ellanora, encumbered by corset, bustle, and unborn baby, is out of breath by the time she is within sight of her house. Ed Noonan, lumbering along with the bulk of the luggage, lends her his arm and they catch up with the other two on the now-quiet stoop.

Annie Spaulding gives a little shriek as the rapping commences again. However this time, it is ordinary knocking, and the women think they hear a familiar voice. Irene picks up the gun and they crowd back down the stairs, allowing Maude to resume her position as guardian of the gate. "Who is it?" she challenges.

"It's Johnny and Ellanora, let us in," comes the welcome reply, and quickly, Maude unbolts and unlocks the door to admit them. Four frightened female voices babble as one, rushing to tell the story of their recent adventure and near-escape. The Kieres weren't even aware that Annie was living in their house until this moment, but that doesn't keep Johnny from snarling, "I wish I had been here. I would have shown them a thing or two." The entire group moves into the warmth of the kitchen, all still talking at once. Ellanora removes her sack coat and gold watch and chain that are pinned to the front of her buff-colored wool suit. Johnny hangs up his dark overcoat and navy pea jacket and starts to unwrap his packages, while Irene sinks into a chair, leaving the old pistol on the table.

This time there is no mistaking when the racket starts again. "For God's sake, don't let him in here!" Annie shrieks. Johnny immediately leaps to his feet and snatches up the gun, while Irene grabs at his arm, imploring, "Don't, John, don't." Impatiently he shakes her off, calling her a fool and, pocketing the firearm, he shouts at Annie, still screaming at the top of her lungs, to be quiet. Mrs. Hanley retreats back upstairs leaving seven men and women thrashing about the small, dimly lit room in wild confusion, while curses and threats of violence intrude from the low steps at the front of the house.

Ellanora stops her husband and with a firm, calm voice, says that she will go and "pacify" the men. From a pocket concealed deep within the folds of her dress, she produces a small ladies' pistol, but evidently thinks better of it and puts it back. Quietly she asks Annie for the cast-iron stove shaker, which the girl finds behind the range, and brandishing this weapon, goes and unlocks the front door, opening it a crack. Annie hides behind the kitchen door, while the others all crowd the back of the hall, craning their necks to see what will happen. They hear the voice of a young man demanding admission and Ellanora's response that it is "too late for visitors" and that he should go home. He starts to shout and she shouts something in return. Muttering, "Let him in, I'll take care of him," Johnny breaks from the little group and rushes to his wife's side, pulling his gun out from his pocket as he goes. There is a small struggle as the two men exchange angry words. Ellanora raises the iron stove shaker above her head and brings it down hard on the person standing just outside, while at the same instant there is a flash and report from a pistol. No one sees what Johnny and Ellanora do next, as Annie's screams rise in the night.

After Fidel Wise passed the Kieres, he continued on until he thought they weren't looking and then rushed down First Street and back up Prison Alley, hoping to get to the boys at Larry Mack's before they did. As he neared the intersection of Second and the Alley he saw Johnny Kiere and James Carrol running towards number 14. The door must have been bolted, as he could plainly hear them knocking and asking to be admitted. Fidel knew he didn't have a moment to lose as he sneaked behind the group on the steps and stole quietly into the saloon. Giles and Charley were busy telling Larry MacNamara all about their adventures that evening, when Fidel informed them that the Kieres had returned. Thinking that this piece of information would convince the two to get out and let the air clear, he was mortified to see that they were merely galvanized into action, both attempting to rush next door and complete the trouble they had started. Fidel managed to stop first one, and then the other, but between the two of them they were able to circumnavigate the little banjo player and array themselves for battle outside. Fidel chased them onto the bordello stoop and fairly attacked Giles Spaulding, grabbing him by the shoulders and wrestling him away from the door.

Now Charley commences his pounding and profanity anew. The noise brings a couple of ladies out onto the steps of the house across the street, and the neighborhood barber, out for a walk and a smoke, pauses at the corner of Warren to watch. As Fidel subdues Giles, the door at Kiere's opens. He hears a woman's voice and then a man's, and sees a man's silhouette. In his excitement, Charley jumps up on the little seat built onto the side of the stoop, giving the two boys in the alley a clear view of the door. The light is faint in the hallway behind the figure, as though it comes from a room way in the back of the house, but there is enough moonlight to see the white-shirted arm and the gun. "Charley will get shot!" Fidel shouts as he releases Giles and rushes towards their friend. Fidel is just an arm's length, just a finger's reach away as the flare and crack of the gunshot rings out, the lead ball tearing into Charley's chest, passing through his lung, and lodging solidly in his spine. Charles Hermance's body trembles with shock. He stumbles off the steps, away from Fidel's grasp and falls headlong onto the stoop of Uriah Hand's carpenter shop two doors away. Fidel sprints after him, while all Giles can do is stand rooted to the spot, calling, "Charley—Charley," in his dull, thick voice. Charley is lying on his back as Fidel reaches him. Tenderly he reaches down and cradles the boy's head, smoothing back his hair and looking into his eyes which are fixed open, but have lost their focus. There is no bleeding. There is no sound. Charles Hermance is dead.

Ellanora walks slowly into the turmoil in the kitchen, staring intently at the iron stove shaker she still holds in her hand. It seems to Maude that she is searching its surface for some trace of blood from the boy who just a moment ago was shouting threats on her doorstep, wondering, perhaps, how so domestic and innocent an instrument could have caused all that damage. Johnny Kiere follows her into the room, breathing hard with—fear? Remorse? Guilt? He looks around at the assembled witnesses and then turns to his wife. "I feel sorry for you, Ellanora," he says theatrically, like an amateur actor in a Christmas pageant, "for you have done the deed. You had better go down and turn yourself in." Ellanora completes her inspection of the stove shaker and turns her gaze to meet her husband's. There is purposeful communication in their looks and, understanding what she must do, she breaks the stare, saying simply, "Yes."

Asking her sister to accompany her, Irene and Ellanora quickly get into outdoor clothes and step through the front door into the growing maelstrom outside. Inflammatory comments concerning the guilt of Johnny Kiere are being muttered by the growing assembly, as the women turn and head for the police station, where they find Officer Shephard eating a very late lunch. Ellanora places her hat on the table, seats herself in a chair, and calmly announces to the startled officer that she has just shot a man, and would he please lock her up?

Punishment and the law weigh heavily as well on the minds of those left inside the house. The group finally manages to quiet Annie's cries and leave her trembling with confusion. She is certain that it is her husband who has been shot and is terrified that somehow she will receive the blame. Passions surge as each person around her is profoundly aware that they, who normally live outside the law, are now involved in a blood-crime, and that soon the pounding on the door will begin again, but this time with the night sticks of the Hudson Police Department. Annie Spaulding doesn't wait for anyone to speak to her and slips quietly away, seeking sanctuary in her mother's home nearby. Young James Carol leaves next, running down to the dock and jumping on the first boat he can find, seeking a hide-out among the disreputables of Kingston, twenty-five miles downriver, while Johnny and his bartender Ed Noonan set about hiding guns and plotting strategies.

Suddenly, Frank Morrison (whom everyone had forgotten about) bursts into the brothel shouting, "Someone's shot Charley Hermance!"

"Is that so?" responds Johnny. "Well, Ellanora did it and it can't be helped."

As has been the case all evening, Fidel Wise seems the only person with a head on his shoulders as he tries to force events into some semblance of sanity. First he makes Giles go for a doctor, while he seeks help from the men in the saloon and later from Officer Hallenbeck, raising the alarm as he goes. A crowd follows along behind as they return to the scene only to discover Irene just returning from having delivered Ellanora into custody. Fidel insists that it is Johnny who is guilty, and Hallenback enters the house. "I didn't do it!," Kiere shouts down from the top of the stairs. "It was my wife! She's gone to turn herself in!" The police officer arrests him anyway, and then, for good measure, Irene as well.

By now Giles has returned in a panic, dragging Dr. Benson, hoping against hope that his friend can still be saved, but the doctor just confirms what everyone else already knows. One group of men carries Charley's body to the home of his father-in-law, who lives nearby, while a runner is dispatched to fetch his wife.

As the alarm spreads throughout the town, Second Street between Prison Alley and Diamond rapidly fills with people. The arrival of the devastated young wife, now widow, inflames the crowd and dozens of men, with a few women watching from the sidelines, start clamoring for the blood of John V. Kiere. Once again, 14 North Second Street comes under siege, with something close to a riot under way when Officers Hallenback, William Brown, and James Cooney appear with the man the crowd is clamoring to lynch. With considerable difficulty, they manage to convey him to the jail where he joins his wife in a small, narrow cell. In short order, officers are sent to pick up French Maude, Ed Noonan, and Frank Morrison, all of whom are jailed as material witnesses. Annie Spaulding is brought in the next day and a detective is sent to find James Carrol, hiding in Kingston. For some reason, Mrs. Hanley escapes notice, possibly because she has managed to get through the entire evening without actually seeing anything. Meanwhile, officers search the Kiere residence and discover two pistols, one large and one small, lying in the bottom of a dresser drawer, covered with an undershirt. Both have a single bullet missing from their chambers.

Christmas Eve, 1876. During the day, there has been such passionate public indignation concerning the crime that even acquaintances of Johnny Kiere are attacked on the streets. In an attempt to keep drunken and potentially violent gangs from forming, Mayor Townsend personally closes all the saloons in town. Even so, at nine o'clock in the evening, a group of young hotheads spreads a false alarm of fire with the intention of drawing out a mob to storm the jail and hang Johnny Kiere. Mayor Townsend, who has less than a week remaining in his term of office, thwarts the effort with the aid of one police officer, and has the three ringleaders thrown into the same jail as their intended victim.

Meanwhile, the Kieres and Irene Brancari sweat in their cells, accused of murder. Irene, responding to hecklers, shouts out the window, "There ain't men enough in Hudson to hang me!" while Ellanora is heard to remark with morbid humour that "hemp makes a nice necktie." Johnny hasn't slept all night. French Maude, continuing her lessons in vice, teaches Annie how to smoke a cigar, while the two of them complain about their rotten luck. Ed and Frank, in cells nearby, are anxious to cooperate in any way they can to save their own necks. As they sit in the dark, the prisoners can just make out the sound of Christmas carols drifting through the air.

*

Monday, February 5, 1877. Justice A. Melville Osborn commences the search for jurors in the Hermance murder trial. The task is not easy, as everyone has been talking about the case for weeks, and the local press has long ago reached a verdict on the guilt of Johnny Kiere, whom they have dubbed "a notorious desperado." Judge Osborn instructs the county clerk to call an additional 100 men from whom to impanel a jury, and the court settles in for a long selection process. Slowly the men are chosen—Rufus Miller, Elkany Decker, Lott Cook, Heiman Pratt, John B.

Skinkle—the list gradually creeps up to the requisite number of 12. The counsel for the defense protests that a published sermon by the Rev. J. C. Hoyt implying the guilt of the defendants will prejudice the jury, but Judge Osborn airily dismisses his concern, remarking dryly that "the citizens of Columbia County are not given to reading sermons." These same citizens fall all over themselves to find reasons why they should be excused, with so many citing ill health that Judge Osborn wonders if a jury will ever be assembled. When Jacob Stuplebeen seeks to be released on the grounds that he is Postmaster of Ghent, he is allowed to "step down and out," but His Honor hisses in an aside to the clerk not to destroy the man's summons as "there might be a change in the list of postmasters."

The trial takes all week. Extra benches and chairs have been borrowed from City Hall, but they are not expected to be enough for the masses of spectators assembling for the social event of the decade. Every day, long before the doors to the courtroom are opened, hordes of people swarm the old, domed courthouse, filling the stairway and vestibule, and forming a mob extending all the way to the gates of the fenced-in square in front. At first, court officers try to impose some order on the chaos by admitting jurors and court personnel early, but that soon proves unworkable, and it is all they can do to weed out the young boys from the crowds storming the stairways. Special considerations are universally granted, however, to the many ladies who attend, decked out in their finest. They are permitted the private use of a side staircase and frequently all legal action comes to a screeching halt as bailiffs are sent scurrying to find extra chairs for the delicate creatures to rest their padded posteriors, while the displaced men stand in the back, jostling for a view. The press is here in full force, with reporters from as far away as Albany and New York City, fully aware that sex and murder sell papers. Overhead, the gallery is reserved for the rabble, which keeps up a lively commentary on the proceedings, calling one court officer "an old turkey" and howling with derisive laughter when told to be quiet.

The prisoners are all seated on chairs in front of the jury, John Kiere in a black frock coat and Ellanora wearing the same fashionable, light-colored dress she wore on the night of the crime. Their four-year-old daughter sits on her lap, but the mother doesn't pay her much attention, distracted as she is by the proceedings. Irene, Maude, Annie, Ed, James, and Frank are there too, trying to look as respectable as possible. Annie wears a black veil in an attempt at modesty, although one observer notes that she appears to be thoroughly enjoying herself as she keeps up a lively conversation with the other women. Because of her "large build" he thinks that she seems much older than her fifteen years. Charles Hermance's widow and mother are present also, strategically placed by the defense table, facing the jury, dressed in deep, black mourning. The Hermances' seven-year-old son sits with them, making the picture of his mother and grandmother's genuine grief that much more poignant.

In his opening statement for the People, District Attorney John B. Longley paints Giles Spaulding as a husband wronged by a young wife who had "so far stepped aside from virtue" as to leave him to reside in Kiere's house, "by common repute... a most infamous place." Charles Hermance was Spaulding's selfless friend, the "honest, sober citizen" who, seeking to rescue a fallen woman, rapped on the whore house door in "an ordinary and orderly manner" when for no reason, a pistol was fired and "Hermance fell reeling to the sidewalk, a corpse."

Twenty-five-year-old J. Rider Cady, acting as counsel for the defense, wonders if the Kiere household was really as "infamous" as claimed, suggesting that Irene Brancari, minding the house for her absent sister, may have merely called some of her female friends over for company late on the Saturday before Christmas. He spends very little time pursuing this theory. More to the point, he illustrates the irresponsible, drunken actions of the men trying to force their way into the house, and claims they brought their fate upon themselves.

One by one, the witnesses are called forth to give their stories. Fidel Wise is relaxed and charming, cracking jokes and making the courtroom laugh. French Maude recounts the fear inside the brothel as Giles Spaulding tried to get in to "get that woman of his'n." Giles, on the other hand, says that he merely rapped lightly on the door with his knuckles, although he may have also "touched it" with his foot. He has trouble remembering a lot of specifics prior to the shooting, and when asked by counsel exactly what he and his friends had been doing in all the saloons they visited that night, he replies incredulously, "We all drinked! At least I know I did."

An argument develops between the woman who wants to be convicted and the witnesses who want to exonerate her. Ellanora takes the stand to insist that she and she alone fired the shot that killed Charley Hermance, and is supported by Johnny's friends, Ed Noonan and James Carrol. Fidel and the women, however, are sure that the husband and not the wife is guilty. Ellanora and Johnny's friends say that Charley smashed the windows on both sides of the door. The police say the glass remains intact. Ellanora and Johnny's friends say that Charley came all the way through the door and struck her. Fidel and the women deny that Charley ever got off the stoop. Ellanora and Johnny's friends say that she ran back to the kitchen, snatched the gun out of Johnny's pocket, then ran back to shoot the boy. Irene and Maude saw Johnny go forward to the door while Ellanora stayed where she was. Ellanora says that it was she, in her buff-colored dress, that Fidel saw in the moonlight, while Johnny was in a dark business suit. The women say they saw Johnny remove his navy pea-coat, leaving him in his white shirt-sleeves, while Fidel recognized Johnny's voice. Everyone saw Ellanora with the stove shaker and everyone saw her with the little pistol. The doctors say a mark on Charley's face could have been made with the kitchen utensil. The police say that the recovered bullet was too big to have been fired from Ellanora's pistol. Everyone saw Ellanora strike with the shaker, but no one can explain how she did this and fired Johnny's heavy gun at the same time. Annie says that she was too busy being hysterical to notice much. Frank was absent, mentally and physically. Giles was too drunk. Johnny never testifies.

The jury is sequestered as soon as the closing arguments are completed. All night they are locked up in the Grand Jury room, occasionally asking the judge for instructions, and arguing so loudly in the hours before dawn that they can be heard in the street. At 8:30 Saturday morning, they are escorted to the General Worth Hotel two blocks away for breakfast. Hundreds of pairs of eyes are glued to the procession as it makes its way back to the deliberation chamber. Finally, after 17 hours of debate, word goes out that they have reached a verdict.

The chaos at the courthouse is replaced with bedlam. One huge crowd masses at the front entrance, while another tries to circumvent it by coming in the back. When the doors are opened, both mobs collide in the middle and create a solid logjam on the stairs. Many intrepid newsmen and court employees avoid the mess by climbing in the windows, but the session must be delayed when it is discovered that one of the judges is trapped in the crush outside. Adding to the mayhem is the news that "Red-Nosed Barney," a notorious pickpocket, has been seen in the vicinity, and the police marshal their meager forces to try to flush out him and his companions.

The first order of business is Irene Brancari, who is also under indictment for murder. All charges against her are dropped because of her help to the prosecution. For a moment she stands a little stunned, and then quietly asks her lawyer if she is free to go where she pleases. On being assured of her liberty, she becomes aware of the melodrama of the situation and throws her hands into the air, shrieking, "My sister! Oh, my poor sister! What will become of her?"

French Maude, standing nearby, rolls her eyes and snarls, "Don't make a fool of yourself."

Johnny Kiere is convicted of second-degree murder. His wife is acquitted of all charges. Nobody is particularly surprised by the verdict. It was hard for anyone to believe that this beautiful young woman could have committed such a bloody act, not only because of the obvious problems with the evidence, but because men of this century frequently have trouble acknowledging that the "weaker sex" can be capable of strength and violence. Beyond that, however, it is apparent to most onlookers that Ellanora is used to taking the lumps for (and sometimes from) her husband, and that she is under his control to the point that she would naturally accept punishment for a crime he committed rather than let him suffer himself. Perhaps these two thought that if they made the killing look like self-defense on the part of a pregnant woman, they would both get off, but no one believes there was that much planning. Ellanora shares the plight of many of her bawdy-house contemporaries. Kate Best, Nell Weeks, Ada Conroy and Annie Spaulding all must suffer the mind-control of a violent, unreasonable man. But then, so must the wife of the respectable Charles Hermance, now doomed to drift about the town in her widow's weeds like some black ghost, searching for her soul.

Judge Osborn, in sentencing Kiere, has this to say about Ellanora:

> Your wife, who was indicted with you, has, by her conduct and her evidence, exhibited an amount of affection for you which has been the wonder... of this whole community. That she should be willing to sacrifice herself either from her own volition or at your suggestion and entreaty to spare your life...furnishes an evidence of womanly heroism and devotion seldom, if ever witnessed before. As we contemplate it, we can almost forgive her for deliberately swearing to an untruth in order to carry out this object and purpose. But truth is mighty

and will prevail. The story was too unreasonable and improbable to be credited by honest and intelligent men.[7]

John V. Kiere is sentenced to life at hard labor at the state penitentiary in Dannemora, New York. He will spend the rest of his days digging iron ore and fashioning nails in the prison shop. It is considered the hardest lock-up in the state and for the first time in the whole proceeding, Ellanora breaks down and cries. Johnny picks up their daughter and they all return to the jail to indulge their emotions. A few days later, just before dawn, Johnny is secretly placed aboard a train heading north. On the way to the station, he is permitted to visit his mother on Front Street, she having been unable or unwilling to go see her son in jail. His wife has spent Johnny's last night in Hudson with him in his little jail cell, and stands forlornly on the platform watching the train disappear in the distance. Ellanora eventually gives up her midnight career, moving in with her in-laws next door to the saloon and supporting herself as a dressmaker. After that, she is lost to history.

During the summer, it is reported that a prostitute named Annie, formerly of Hudson but now living in Albany, has inherited $6,000, a veritable fortune in an era when the average worker makes about $300 per year. It could be Saucy Nellie, whose real name is Ann, or one of Mary Mackey's "stable," or one of Hat Benton's, but it is just a little more than likely that it is a buxom, teenaged girl who has finally realized her dreams of a glamorous life, and has truly escaped Giles, Hudson, and some unpleasant memories, at least for a little while.

Ten days after Johnny Kiere is convicted, a stranger

from Washington Hollow in Dutchess County presents himself at the Hudson police station. He is searching for his nineteen-year-old daughter named Phebe who has disappeared from home after taking up with a local man who was "her seducer and abductor, and the cause of [her] sorrow and trouble."[8] Rumor has it that she is living in one of Hudson's houses of ill repute and the father, anxious and sad, merely wants his daughter to come home. Police Justice Overhiser dispatches Officer Winslow to investigate, and before long the girl is located at the bagnio of William Leonard on Diamond Street. Father and daughter are peacefully reunited and reconciled, boarding the 11:28 train for Washington Hollow and home. In this case, a murder was not necessary.

4: THE LAW

JOHN KIERE'S FRIENDS DIDN'T FARE TOO WELL IN 1877.[1] Sod Kelly was sentenced to six months in prison for assault. The proprietor of Larry Mack's was stabbed and seriously wounded at the county fair. And Ed Noonan must have been remembering his weeks in jail as a material witness when he slung a stone at Officer Vincent, hitting him in the head. That same day Police Justice Overhiser had Noonan jailed in the Albany prison for two months.

1877 was a banner year for the Hudson Police Department, however. It had only been in existence for four years but the general crime rate had fallen dramatically, and the Kiere episode was their crowning achievement. Certainly there were other crimes in 1877, like thefts and rapes. In the summer, a black woman was "ravished" near the train tracks by two white men. The rapists were soon caught and harshly dealt with. In the autumn, Coon Mundy was arrested for hitting his girlfriend and killing her, but he said the beating really didn't amount to much as "she was used to it."

However, most of the officers' time was spent arresting drunks and providing lodging for some of the armies of homeless tramps that roamed the nation in an era of virtually nonexistent social services. 1877 saw Belle Williams run in a couple of times for using obscene language on the Sabbath, and one spring day, a 14-year-old boy thought it would be funny to shave a cross into his friend's short haircut. He got two days in jail for blasphemy. And then there was the time officers were called to control an excited crowd which had gathered to see a giant tapeworm that Dr. Logan had removed from Mrs. Sarah McGuire of Albany. So many people wanted to look at the thing, they had to take it to the big auditorium above City Hall where, according to the report, "the reptile... was alive for over an hour after it was removed from the lady."

Before 1873, when eight men were issued blue uniforms, tall hats, and nightsticks, the city had languished under largely ineffective law enforcement systems. At first, the Proprietors had established a "night watch," which existed primarily to patrol the town for fires. The Watch had extremely limited authority and when they discovered an emergency situation, basically all they could do was scream for help. If it was a big emergency, they could scream louder. They couldn't make formal arrests, so they were not very effective at stopping crime. Since much of

Hudson burned down several times before 1840, they were not all that effective at stopping fires either.

Eventually the Night Watch was eliminated and for over 40 years, what was known as the Constable System was in effect. Every year, one man from each of Hudson's four electoral wards was elected to keep the peace. These constables, sometimes supplemented with additional members when the Common Council saw fit, could make arrests, but only after first obtaining a warrant. Without that paper they were powerless, and even in those cases where they actually witnessed a crime in progress they would have to depend on a citizen to swear out an official complaint before action could be taken. Hudson's citizenry was notoriously uncooperative in such matters, not that the citizenry appreciated the constables' efforts, either. In an emergency, the first trick was to find an officer, since they were not required to make any kind of patrol and there was no central police station. Hudsonians learned early that a good place to look was at a saloon's gaming table or sometimes even a brothel, where the lawmen were undoubtedly conducting in-depth investigations of the criminal element in his lair. As for this criminal element, they soon learned that many constables were susceptible to bribery because of their lousy pay.[2] Hudson remained a criminal's playground, partially because the constables couldn't stop them, and partially because the streets were so dark, no one could see them anyway.

Hudson's silly system of lighting street lamps only when there was no moon was actually a fairly common practice in eighteenth-century America, but by the Civil War it had become hopelessly outdated. Even on nights when the lamps were lit, they were extinguished before midnight, just as the illicit fun was getting into full swing. For decades there were calls from the more enlightened for proper illumination, but there were years when the penny-wise citizenry couldn't even be coerced to approve funding to maintain the inadequate lighting they already had. In 1855, when the Mayor announced that the lighting budget would be $1,200, Hudson's citizens were appalled and voted down the tax needed to produce so vast a sum. That year the lamps weren't lit at all, resulting in a dramatic increase in crime, including one robbery so serious that the town was compelled to offer a reward of $300, thus reducing Hudson's 1855 budget savings to only $900. As absurd as that was, twelve years later this exact scenario was played out all over again.[3]

If all this wasn't enough, there were so many jail breaks that the structure was deemed virtually worthless. The masonry lock-up behind the courthouse wasn't any more secure than the old log prison that the determined Dutchman drilled his way through in the 1780s. During one week in the 1860s, a pair of incarcerated thieves was discovered first breaking a hole through the wall, then removing the bars on their window, and finally chopping a hole in the roof. Although they were caught each time, others were more successful. The editor of the *Evening Register* expressed the opinion of many when he wrote:

> The fact is, murderers, robbers, pickpockets, assassins, and criminals of every dye are invited to operate in our city by the inducements of dark streets, an inefficient police force, and a frail structure for the keeping of prisoners. It is useless to attempt to

conceal the fact that there is no security for life or property in our midst, except through such precaution as individual citizens adopt for their own protection.[4]

Since neither the night watch, the constables, nor threats of prison were able to control criminal activity, some in the town were anxious to have a real municipal police force like New York City had formed in 1845, but, typically, no one wanted to pay for it. Time and again the voters of Hudson were asked to approve a budget that would provide for the law enforcement agency, and time and again the voters of Hudson turned it down. (Hudson's total tax levy in 1865 was $14,000, ridiculously low, even for those days.)[5] Referring to the general business climate, a commentator in 1871 chided an

"element among [Hudson's] wealthier citizens... averse to investing their hoarded wealth [and who are out to] discourage with a singular selfishness and a jealousy the disposition in others to reap the benefit growing out of judicious enterprise and industry, and which their own illiberality alone prevents their enjoying."[6]

In other words, Hudsonians were cheap. Not that there was no industry. Hudson had an iron works, a carriage maker's, breweries, and a host of other manufactories. But the commercial vision of the founding Quakers had deteriorated into a nasty, penny-pinching, short-sighted philosophy of instant gratification. Whores, thugs, and gunfights on the Sabbath couldn't convince Hudson's merchants to help raise the money to address

Hudson's problems. In 1872, when there were only 20 Quakers left,[7] there was a rash of daring Warren Street robberies grievous enough to cause the police measure to be rushed through. The Hudson Police Department was at last a reality. However the townspeople still refused to finance street lighting, a board of education, new school buildings, a library, a new fire engine. . . .

The handling of the John Kiere incident was a major boost to the morale, not only of the fledgling Police Department, but also to those who were sick of living in a town known as "the most lawless city on the River."[8] For decades people had placidly accepted the existence of their home-grown vice business as something beyond their control, but when Johnny Kiere killed Charles Hermance, the town was galvanized into indignant reaction. However, it was not the city's government (which had control over the police), but a newly formed private citizens' organization called the "Law and Order Alliance" that worked with the force to bring about the first wholesale effort to clean up Hudson.

Mostly, the police action was quiet. William Leonard was sentenced to six months at hard labor soon after young Phebe was rescued from his House. Hat Benton and her girls were brought in, her mother fighting and filling the air with obscenities. Hat was convicted and fined. So were two of her white customers, perhaps only because they consorted with black women.

Mary Mackey was quietly picked up at her saloon at Front and Union and was eventually sentenced to six months at hard labor, possibly because she had the largest bawdy house in town. This didn't stop her operation, however, as business just continued under the direction of

Julia Bennet, one of her veteran ladies. One night during the summer, the place was "pulled" by a force of police officers, and seven men, in various stages of undress, crashed out the windows and ran in every direction as the police rounded up Julia and two other women. Hester, who had only been out of jail a month, was particularly irate with her arresting officer and got to join her boss, Mary, for a six-month stint of her own. Anna, while not immediately charged, was chased half-way across the state so she could be brought back to testify against her co-workers. Material witnesses seemed not to fare any better than the accused in those days.

Nell Weeks may have gotten her jewelry back after Saucy Nellie absconded with it to Connecticut, but in the post-Kiere moral sweep, the Law and Order Alliance targeted her house on Diamond Street and she soon found herself in the county jail behind the courthouse. Always resourceful, Nell took up with one Hiram Lifelight, serving time for horse theft. Many of the prisoners were given little chores to perform: One night, the jailer gave Hiram the key to the front door so the convict could get out to take care of the sheriff's horses, while the jailer himself went home to his supper, no one thinking it odd to assign a horse thief such a task. For some reason the turnkey was surprised (or said he was) when he found Nell and Hiram gone in the morning.

All told, the Law and Order Alliance assisted the Hudson Police in closing at least four bawdy houses, but there were still others that remained unmolested. Most of those convicted were merely fined, and almost all were back in business before a year had passed. At an official banquet that fall, a toast was made "to the Twin Sisters,

Dutchess and Columbia [counties]." A newsman wryly noted that it should have been made instead to "the Sin Twisters."[9]

By 1879, morale among the police, faced as they were with bad pay, little moral support from the government they worked for, and seeing that all their righteous actions had basically been for naught, was reported to be badly deteriorating. The four men who were assigned to night duty habitually deserted their posts by midnight and someone composed a popular street ditty, "Whoever saw a policeman at two o'clock in the morning?"[10] The Law and Order Alliance's high-minded crusade was a forgotten fad.

1889. New York State raised the age of sexual consent to 16. Electric street lights were at long last installed in Hudson and soon there would be a new mandatory education law, reducing the numbers of unruly youngsters in the streets, and causing the general crime rate to go down. However, the new generation of Diamond Street prostitutes and madams largely thumbed their noses at police activity and the officers basically gave up trying. A bawdy house had to become a major public nuisance before any official move was made against it. Occasionally, a patron, after having been robbed, beaten up, or just having his pride wounded, would make a complaint, but all charges were invariably dropped as the good citizen, realizing the social implications involved, would fail to appear in court. At any rate, simple vice cases ranked lowest in priority in Hudson's overloaded justice system, leaving bawdy housekeepers to operate with virtual impunity.[11] In 1894 Mayor Miller stated that the Department had "fallen into utter disrepute"[12] and created a three-man police commission in an attempt to improve efficiency. They immediately ordered all the brothel owners to close or face prosecution. Presumably they all closed. Presumably they all opened again by Thanksgiving. The police still got no respect.

In the late 1890s, a Democratic mayor appointed a local Democratic Party official to the police commission who, according to one writer, immediately set about turning the commission into an "annex of the Democratic political machine."[13] Payoffs and bribes became commonplace in both political parties by the turn of the century, which attracted to the community "more than its share of criminal parasites and [fostered] increased criminal activity."[14]

The citizens were roused to action once again. The *Evening Register* blasted Mayor Harvey in 1901 for not shutting down Diamond Street and warned that state law could thwart the political machine and reach "any city official."[15] Vigilante groups were formed to stop crime and "break up sinful abodes."[16] One band was made up of whites whose sole purpose was to harass blacks. But when one of the intended victims fought back, killing his attacker, public opinion came down largely in the black man's favor, criticizing the police for allowing the white thugs to operate, and lambasting the courts because gang members had previously been brought before a judge and released. In 1901 the *Hudson Republican*, in an article entitled "Decency in Hudson," accused Police Commissioner Arkison of protecting the disorderly houses, going on to say that if he stood aside, the "filthy nests" could be cleaned out.[17] The Commissioner responded to the press in a typically political fashion.

"Two Bad Wenches Jailed" ran the headline in the *Evening Register* for July 20, 1901. Two young women had been arrested for "unbecoming" behavior. Teenaged Fan was described as a "young colored wench." Twenty-eight-year-old Sarah was described as a "rather good-looking colored woman." She seems to have made quite an impression on a certain male newspaper reporter. Fan was immediately sent to the House of Refuge for three years where, it was hoped, she would learn to be a good wench. Sarah supposedly had been part of a "lewd orgy in which she was one of the chief participants" at the saloon in Arthur Trebilcox's Adirondack Hotel on the corner of Third and Diamond. Visions of unbridled licentiousness must have filled Hudson imaginations, as it was darkly rumored that Miss Sarah had "danced the St. Louis," a sinister accusation, undoubtedly, to Victorian ears.

Two days later, a whole group of black men and women was brought in, accused of being prostitutes and their customers. On July 31, another black woman and one Mrs. Mary Fahey, whom neighbors charged with being a "disorderly person," were detained. Mrs. Fahey went to jail for six months for "using foul language and drunkenness," but most of the other men and women arrested during this "sweep" were released for lack of evidence. The judge, exasperated by what he perceived as a sloppy police investigation, declared that convictions should have been easy to obtain, remarking that the bawdy houses had been operating in Hudson "since I was born."[17]

Meanwhile, Arthur Trebilcox, who stood accused of keeping a "disorderly hotel," claimed that he was totally unaware of what this "bad wench" was doing in his saloon while he was present. The white, male taxpayer was acquitted. Miss Sarah, meanwhile, was convicted of conducting a "lewd performance." The poor, black prostitute was put away for the standard six months. Once again the newspapers protested, denouncing the verdict as a travesty of justice and calling for the dismissal of the presiding judge.[19] But nothing much changed and everyone soon forgot about the whole thing. The commissioner remained firmly in office. So did the Diamond Street madams.

For the next 50 years or so, the little game continued. One mayor cleaned up, the next one was denounced by the press as corrupt. Some commissioners were decent, some bad, others worse. Police morale would be reported up, and then reported down, and then up again. And every now and again a mayor would pompously declare that Hudson "has too long suffered from the bad reputation of being a free and easy place"[20] or some such thing, while bad wenches continued to dance the St. Louis just a block from City Hall.

In 1911 two Hudson police officers were stabbed and seriously wounded while trying to arrest a couple of suspects in a series of robberies and assaults. For a moment, the force seemed united in a fervent desire to purge the town of vice once and for all. However, this time it was Hudson's populace that stepped in to hamper the well-intentioned action, publicly ridiculing the police for even thinking they could end the prostitution and illegal gambling, so deeply entrenched had they become. In frustration, Police Commissioner Coffin wrote an open letter to the people of Hudson asking for public cooperation in closing the "disorderly houses, veritable pest holes of disease and crime... running openly and flaunting their vice."[21] He also described the evils of poker-playing for money and "lottery devices" in cigar stores and saloons. For a while this tactic appeared to work and Hudson was said to begin to resemble other small towns, but in 1915 the mayoral administrations changed and the bawdy roller coaster plunged downward once again. That year, a cabaret, "notorious for the lewdness of the performances it staged,"[22] prompted an anti-cabaret ordinance. The papers said the mayor was making an empty political gesture, a new police commissioner was said to be protecting the brothels, et cetera, et cetera, et cetera.

1918 brought Prohibition and a whole new dimension to Hudson's nighttime diversions. Suddenly, the dozens of saloons and taverns, all of them with some kind of gambling, and a few of them with ladies for hire upstairs, became illegal themselves. Speakeasies sprouted up everywhere, like Macabee's Hall on the top floor of the building on the corner of Fourth and Warren, or the place below Third that had previously been a shoe store, or Little Red's at the corner of First Street. At Andrew Wise's you could get a beer for ten cents, and Hallenbeck's Saloon hid behind a supposedly empty storefront. But even children knew that if you pressed the "secret" button under the window, Mr. Hallenbeck would come from the back to let you in. The "legitimate" bars, selling insipid, non-alcoholic beer, could instantly produce a bottle of the real thing if asked properly, although, in those days, anything with a kick tasted good. When a bootlegger forgot to deliver his shipment of liquor to the speakeasy where Leonard White was bartender, Mr.

White simply filled empty bottles with water and continued making "gin" and tonics. He claimed his customers got just as drunk as usual.

The brewery producing Evan's Ale, one of Hudson's larger employers, went out of business, leaving a big, empty building and dozens of unemployed workers. Shadowy tenants moved in, manufacturing non-alcoholic alcohol that tasted suspiciously like whiskey. The underground brewery on Mill Street was truly underground, a tunnel being dug two blocks to a building on the corner of Second and Diamond. From there, the homemade beer would be distributed, the tunnel serving as a naturally refrigerated storage place. If that wasn't enough, the hills and even many of Hudson's tiny back yards hummed with the sounds of stills dripping homemade brew, Hudson residents trolling the alleys looking for potato peels, old apples, anything fermentable that they could make into alcohol. Mountain farmers would make applejack by freezing barrels of hard cider in the cold Catskill winters, and then retrieving the core of unfrozen liquor to be sold to bootleggers for distribution.

The Law was something that no one could afford to ignore. A truck driver set off late one night in the early 1920s with a shipment from the underground distillery. As he drove out the top end of Warren Street, he was startled to see a strange man jump up on the runningboard and thrust a gun through the window, forcing him to return to the factory. Seeing the truck, the workmen opened the gates, allowing hidden federal marshals to swarm in. The employees were rounded up and the place was shut down. It was an action worthy of "The Untouchables."

The local police were active too. According to one speakeasy owner, every week there would be a sharp rap on the back door and the police chief himself would be found on the threshold. Silently, he would perform a quaint ceremony which involved turning his back to the owner and thrusting his right hand out behind him. Apparently, the chief felt that if he didn't actually see a bribe occur, it hadn't really happened. A state prohibition agent lived in an apartment on Warren Street, wedged in between two active speakeasies. His presence had no effect on business whatsoever.

The law wasn't the only thing tavern-owners had to worry about. Many a new bar in Hudson would receive visits from groups of tough-looking young men who would first order a beer and then spit it out all over the floor exclaiming, "This stuff stinks! From now on, you're ordering your beer from Mr. Diamond!" or something equally subtle. The brew they provided wasn't very good, but for some reason, Mr. Diamond's beer became very popular, nearly replacing O'Connell's which had previously been forced on Hudson by the Albany family of that name. Legs Diamond, the famous gangster, had his headquarters across the river and could supply whatever was needed to slake a body's thirst. In nearby Kingston, Legs made so much illegal hooch that he simply had a liquor pipeline run through the city's sewers, transporting the stuff from his distilleries to the riverside and boats waiting to supply the nation, whether it liked it or not.

Not everyone in Hudson wanted to sell Legs Diamond's second-rate stuff, however. One bartender on 7th Street responded to Legs's men by going after them with a pool cue, badly damaging their faces. They left, and soon after, so did the bartender, as his boss wasn't anxious to have Legs Diamond's boys returning to shoot up the place. Poke Wright, a handsome and promising young Hudson boxer, hung out with the fast crowd from the other side of the river but somehow crossed his new friends. One night he received a mysterious invitation to drive out to Kinderhook Lake, and the next morning his bullet-riddled body was found propped up against the main door of the Hudson Hospital. Another young local man was noticed cheerfully striding up Warren Street lugging a large violin case. A friend, knowing the boy didn't play an instrument, asked to see what was in the box. Grinning proudly, the young man revealed a shiny, new tommy gun. He had borrowed it from a visiting gangster to show to his buddies, proving that life really does imitate bad movies.

Gambling flourished in the speakeasies, with slot machines and gaming tables, and just about every store and business participated in the numbers racket. One Hudson entrepreneur maintained slot machines all over the area, until he received a visit from some dangerous looking violin players with a message. Mr. Diamond, it seemed, wanted a part of the slot machine business and had declared that now only his devices would be allowed in the joints on his side of the river. Remembering Poke Wright, the Hudson entrepreneur decided this was a dandy idea, and asked for a day or two for him to retrieve his equipment. "Oh, those are Mr. Diamond's slot machines now!" he was told.

In 1920, the Police Chief and the head of the Police Commission attempted to stave off public criticism by making a very showy raid on a Diamond Street saloon where gambling was "suspected" to be taking place. Investigating "undercover" in a public taxicab, the two, who could not have failed to be recognized by most people in town, entered the establishment and arrested the owner, seizing as evidence a formidable piece of gambling equipment—a card table. The newspaper snidely lauded the men for at last discovering a place apparently known to everyone but them, but lamented their use of a taxicab to reach a gambling den three blocks from the police station. Perhaps suspecting that something was going on, the common council requested the police commission to report on actions against other gambling operations in the city. The commissioners were told that "the matter was looked into and no violations found."[23] A police officer insisted that there were plenty of violations found and submitted his own report, but not only did the chief refuse to accept it, the man was reprimanded for impertinence.[24]

1921 and the mayor changes, the police commission is re-structured, and the police force is reported as being "totally demoralized"[25]—again. Soon, the authority to close the haunts of gamblers, bootleggers, and prostitutes on their own initiative is removed from the ordinary patrolmen, those decisions becoming the exclusive purview of the chief and mayor. Some officers grumble, to no avail, that they are being forced to break the law by not suppressing crime when they see it.[26] Meanwhile, the newspaper continues to complain about illegal gambling and says that "in every soldier's home in the country, Hudson was being heralded for its bawdy houses."[27] Of course that was not true. Sailors heralded Hudson, too.

It wasn't just servicemen out for a good time who were talking about the little town with the big red light district.

In a confidential report to Governor Franklin D. Roosevelt dated February 27, 1930, investigators stated that in 1928 there were nine "openly conducted brothels" in Hudson. By 1929, that number had increased to 15 "houses of assignation and prostitution," including one hotel, the main business of which was "the use of women of ill fame." Hudson had been under the scrutiny of state lawmakers for some time, for while Albany and neighboring Troy certainly had notorious sin markets of their own, they were a little too close to home for a politician concerned with his reputation. Legend has it that legislative sessions in the Capital would be cut short on Fridays so the lawmakers could catch the train for Hudson and a little sex and relaxation.

The 1930s saw important new developments in Hudson's vice industry. The repeal of Prohibition in 1932 allowed all the speakeasies to come out in the open, which they did with a vengeance. By the end of the decade there were supposedly nearly 65 bars in town, and a popular weekend activity was to tour all the joints, competing to see who could drink a beer in each. The winner was allowed to pass out in the place of his choice. Still-illegal gambling parlours and horserooms did a booming business with the aid of paid drivers bringing in customers from New York, and Western Union ticker-tape machines bringing in the latest results from race tracks around the country. There was one lasting change that the politicians were able to bring about, however. Diamond Street, home to fancy ladies, naughty women, and bad wenches for 135 years had finally been eliminated forever: The name had been changed to Columbia Street.

True to form, there was the usual revolving door of reformers and connivers in town government. Brothel owners had to be prepared to close with each change of administration as they scrambled to curry favor with the new powers at City Hall. In 1932, Mayor Archibald Best once again tried to clean up the town by simply ordering all the madams and their hired help to lock up and leave Hudson forever. Sure enough, at the appointed hour there was an orderly procession of well-dressed ladies making their way by taxi or on foot down to the old train station, accompanied by delivery men and carts with mounds of trunks and hat boxes. All that was needed was the arrival of the Queen Mary to complete the illusion of the embarkation on a glamorous transatlantic crossing. The train arrived, good-byes were completed, and the women departed with much fluttering of handkerchiefs and blowing of kisses. Some cynics have said that they returned by the next train. Undoubtedly they waited at least a week. Maybe two.

Hudsonians did not seem very concerned about prostitution in general, however. While the police may not have been vigilant in rooting out vice, they were very energetic in suppressing ordinary crime, and people were relieved to be free of the kind of lawlessness brought about by the likes of John Kiere and Arthur Trebilcox. Early in 1931, a special grand jury was convened to look into crime in the city, and a report was duly presented to Supreme Court Justice Daniel V. McNamee. Most of it dealt with illegal gambling in very familiar terms, talking of slot machines in basements and the niceties of the "Lucky 50" numbers system as opposed to the "Havana Lottery." Barely 100 words were devoted to prostitution, however, the opinion being that although sex was for sale in Hudson, sex was for sale everywhere, and what could you do? It ended with a tepid recommendation that the Public Safety Commission, Hudson's moral watchdog, "renews its efforts to suppress such crime insofar as the same is physically possible." Bootlegging, still illegal in 1931, wasn't even mentioned.[28]

Sometime in the 1930s a Hudson mayor simply gave up even pretending to prosecute prostitution and went to the other extreme, virtually making commercial sex another department of city government. Perhaps he hoped that a properly managed business would police itself. Perhaps he looked to money from the large numbers of visiting men to spur the depressed local economy. Whatever the reasons, Columbia Street became very orderly, although not exactly legal. At least two local doctors were assigned the official task of visiting the houses once a week to test the girls for venereal disease and issue color-coded cards verifying their state of health—white for "clean," brown for "infected." On a regular basis, Hudson police officers made visits to each of the brothels to check the cards; the holders of brown ones reported to the chief and were sent out of town. They would also take a weekly "census," noting population of each house and making sure the new girls understood the rules.[29] For their part, the madams were more scrupulous than ever in keeping their employees in order and not becoming a nuisance to the town. They also made a point of giving their policemen little gifts of money for their troubles.

A truly bizarre situation developed in 1936 when the bordello at 354 Columbia was raided. The police chief and several officers testified at the madam's trial, all of them freely admitting being acquainted with the woman and knowing her profession. The chief even went so far as to state that he knew her because he collected her health cards every week. The others blithely talked of making patrols on Columbia Street, gathering health cards and "census" information at the other houses.

Officers depicted the scene that night, the street crowded with cars and men looking for action. They carefully described entering the house, discovering three women attempting to hide in specially built secret closets that many brothels had, five men trying to climb out the windows, and the madam openly confessing her guilt. The arresting officers recalled starting for the station with the entire crowd, but "somehow," two of the women and four of the men escaped during the two-block walk, leaving the 30-year-old madam and a poor, hapless barber from Poughkeepsie to be locked up. No one thought any of this was strange. No one questioned why law-enforcement officers were on such familiar terms with madams and prostitutes. Perhaps most importantly, no one asked why on earth this house was raided in the first place, while all the others were left alone. After an exhausting 45-minute deliberation, the jury announced they couldn't reach a verdict. The case was set aside.[30] The lady was still in business years later.

May 1, 1938, the mayor abolishes the public safety commission, while it is also reported that there are still 15 whore houses operating openly.[31] The furious ex-commissioners publicly demand that a raid take place. They are ignored.

A 1940s Fourth of July parade as it starts down the upper end of Columbia Street. *Courtesy of Mr. Bruce Bohnsack.*

Getting ready for a 1940s soap box derby. *Courtesy of Mr. Bruce Bohnsack.*

Some of the homes of the "quality" lining lower Warren Street. *Photo by author.*

The Central House Hotel, scene of the "Sunday Riot." *Courtesy of Hudson Public Library.*

Kate Best's bawdy house was later occupied by Mrs. Ray Church, and finally Carol Desmond. The building housing City Hall and the police station looms in the background. *Photo by author.*

Young men of leisure relaxing on the veranda of a Hudson
mansion in the 1870s. *Courtesy of Hudson Public Library.*

The City Hall/Opera House (photo circa 1880) housed the police station for nearly 100 years. Note the public pump in the foreground. *Courtesy of Mr. Bruce Bohnsack.*

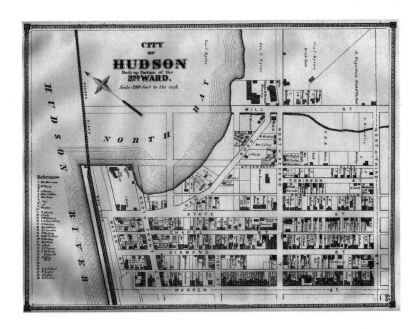

Ellanora Kiere's neighborhood in 1875.
Courtesy of Columbia County Historical Society.

Central Square in the 1870s. Horse manure sometimes was so deep it was hard to tell the street was paved. *Courtesy of Hudson Public Library.*

Kiere's saloon was in the Front Street building on the right. Mary Mackey's saloon and bawdy house was in the building on the left. *Photo by author.*

Kiere's bordello was on the right, in what was then 14 North
Second. Larry Mack's saloon was in building on the left, where
Andrew and Irene Brancari also lived. *Photo by author.*

Crowds reached all the way to the Courthouse gate to see the Kiere trial. *Courtesy of Hudson Public Library.*

Hudson police in the early days. *Courtesy of Hudson Public Library.*

Hudson police officers in front of the City Hall/Police Station in 1931. *From a private collection.*

Patrons of Macabee's Hall, one of Hudson's most popular speakeasies, were identified through the classic peephole. *Photo by author.*

This 1931 aerial picture of Hudson was the only photo that could be found of the Block in its heyday. Note High School on the right. Mansion House is the large flat-roofed building on lower left. From *Hudson From the Air, 1931.*

The Block in 1992. Just a bit more run-down than in 1950. Mae Gordon's was at #352 (extreme right). To the left, at #350, Ma Brown kept a brothel with a small bar/restaurant. Further to the left, slightly set back from the street, was the Chicken Shack. Further down was Vera Faith's and Mae Healy's. The Mansion House was torn down in the 1960s. *Photo by author.*

Evelyn White's Hollowville pleasure palace in 1993. It once had fine antiques and black velvet on the walls. *Photo by author.*

Customers usually went around to the back door. This 1961 photo shows the rear of some houses on The Block. *Courtesy of Hudson Public Library.*

Warren Street in the 1950s. *Courtesy of Mr. Bruce Bohnsack.*

At Spook Rock. *From a private collection.*

A Hudson madam in her underwear. 1920s cheesecake. *From a private collection.*

A Hudson working girl and an unidentified friend. *From a private collection.*

A Hudson madam dresses for a swim. *From a private collection.*

A Hudson madam in repose. *From a private collection.*

A Hudson working girl on holiday. *From a private collection.*

In the kitchen of a Hudson bawdy house. *From a private collection.*

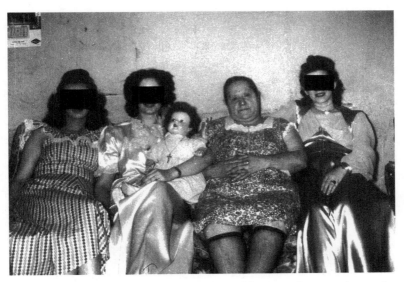

A month before the raid. A madam and her employees, dressed for work. *From a private collection.*

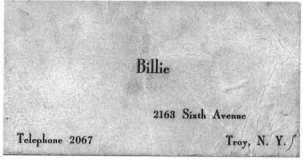

Prostitutes' business cards. Mae's calling card advertised her "beauty parlors" in Hudson and Albany. Note "Columbia" is misspelled. *From a private collection.*

DEPARTMENT OF PUBLIC SAFETY
BUREAU OF HEALTH
ALBANY, N. Y.
LABORATORY REPORT

DR. Padula   DATE Oct.16,1923

NAME May Gordon

WIDAL TEST _____

SPUTUM FOR TUBERCLE BACILLI_____

SMEAR FOR GONOCOCCI. MORPHOLOGICALLY____

FOR SYPHILIS:_____

WASSERMANN TEST : Negative

PRECIPITIN (KAHN) TEST : Negative

Bender Hygienic Laboratory,
ELLIS KELLERT, M. D.
DIRECTOR.

DEPARTMENT OF PUBLIC SAFETY
BUREAU OF HEALTH
ALBANY, N. Y.
LABORATORY REPORT

DR. H.Van Loon   DATE Oct. 16,1924

NAME Mary Stephen

WIDAL TEST_____

SPUTUM FOR TUBERCLE BACILLI_____

SMEAR FOR GONOCOCCI, MORPHOLOGICALLY__ Negative

FOR SYPHILIS:_____

WASSERMANN TEST :_____

PRECIPITIN (KAHN) TEST :_____

BENDER HYGIENIC LABORATORY
JAMES R. LISA, M. D.
DIRECTOR

Working girls got a V.D. test once a week, as did this woman, using two of her many aliases. *From a private collection.*

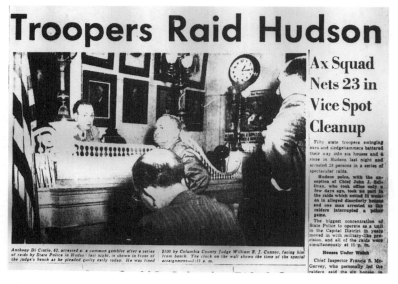

Troopers Raid Hudson

Ax Squad Nets 23 in Vice Spot Cleanup

Fifty state troopers swinging axes and sledgehammers battered their way into six houses and a store in Hudson last night and arrested 23 persons in a series of spectacular raids.

Hudson police, with the exception of Chief John J. Sullivan, who took office only a few days ago, took no part in the raids which netted 21 women in alleged disorderly houses and one man arrested as the raiders interrupted a poker game.

The biggest concentration of State Police to operate as a unit in the Capital District in years moved in with military-like precision, and all of the raids were simultaneously at 11 p. m.

Houses Under Watch

Chief Inspector Francis S. McGarvey, who personally led the raiders said the six houses in

Anthony Di Cintio, 42, arrested as a common gambler after a series of raids by State Police in Hudson last night, is shown in front of the judge's bench as he pleaded guilty early today. He was fined $100 by Columbia County Judge William E. J. Connor, facing him from bench. The clock on the wall shows the time of the special arraignment—1:15 a. m.

The Knickerbocker News, Saturday, June 24, 1950, Albany, NY. The host of a pinochle game was the only individual pictured in the press following the arrests on the night of June 23, 1950.

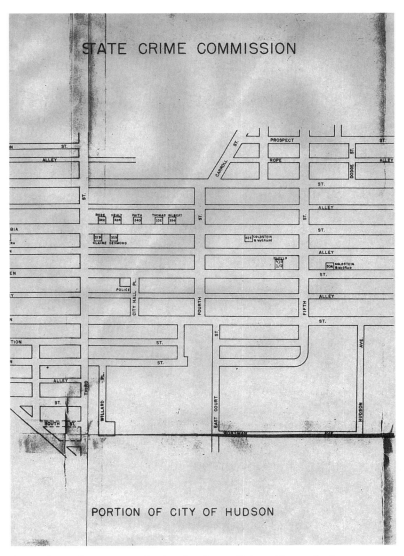

A section of a map made for the State Crime Commission hearings in 1951 showing raid sites. *Courtesy of New York State Library, Albany.*

Upstairs in this garage on the 200 block of Columbia Street (pictured here in the 1950s) was the last site of the famous floating crap game. *Courtesy of Mr. Bruce Bohnsack.*

Mae Healy operated a bordello here, sponsored by a local V.I.P., in the 1940s. When shut down on June 23, 1950, State troopers found two Hudson cops inside. *Photo by author.*

State Police destroying illegal pinball machines used for
gambling in the late 1950s. *Courtesy of Mr. Bruce Bohnsack.*

The Governor's Crime Commission, Hudson, 1951. Judge
Proskauer is in the center of the front row. *Courtesy of Mr. Bruce
Bohnsack.*

Inside the Hudson police station in the 1950s. *Courtesy of Mr. Bruce Bohnsack.*

Old reputations die hard. A Hudson bar, popular in the late-1970s. *Photo by author.*

Local citizens express their opinions on the subject of a 1991 police scandal. *Photo by author.*

5: THE BLOCK

❖

HARLEM, NEW YORK CITY, THE 1940'S.[1] Annabelle worries about her children. The Big City breeds all sorts of problems, especially for teenagers, and the deeply religious woman wants to save them from unnecessary troubles and temptations. She doesn't like the looks of some of her son's friends and she wants her daughters to marry nice boys. Her first grandson is still almost a baby, but already the pressures of the City have colored his young life: another child has stolen his bicycle and broken his heart. Annabelle longs for them to have space and trees and something more than their crowded Manhattan apartment. She prays she can provide her son and daughters with a better life than she and her husband, Richard, have had, in a wholesome place where they will be surrounded by good, decent people. There is a little town she knows of. It is a friendly community, with clean air, surrounded by beautiful, green fields. Richard has been up there looking around and has found a house that they can afford on a quiet, sleepy street. A house of their own! On a little street called Columbia! In a beautiful town called Hudson! Why, it's almost like moving to the country!

The family and furniture arrive one day in a battered old truck. The house is old, sitting right on the sidewalk, but boasts 17 rooms and a pretty backyard where they can plant vegetables and flowers. The mother unpacks as the children begin to get acclimated. They have never seen anything quite like this place. The town is so old-fashioned, laughably small. Almost all the stores are on one main street, and there is only one high school, just outside of town surrounded by fields. City Hall and the police station both share a building, which also houses a public auditorium. There are just three little movie houses and no big buildings of any kind. There is no denying that the place is pretty, with its quaint houses and beautiful views of the Hudson River and the Catskill Mountains beyond, but after living in New York City, the streets feel unnaturally empty. Except on weekends.

The first weekend in their new house and the family is charmed by the activity around them. The little street is full of cars and people and seems more like home. From a nearby tavern, they can hear the beautiful voices of women singing popular songs. Some people sit on stoops or in automobiles visiting with friends. There are dozens of men just walking around, including a small number of black men, their dungarees heavily starched in their version of formal wear. From behind the windows of neighboring houses, there is conversation and laughter. The daughters are delighted ("Ooh! It's just like a parade, Mama!") but curious about the hubbub outside. They assume that all the traffic is for Jack's Bar next door, although it does seem a little odd that such a little hole in the wall like Jack's could bring out all these people.

Successive weekends and the New Yorkers are increasingly puzzled by life in the little town. During the week, Hudson is so quiet, the people so nice, yet the weekend crowds on their narrow street seem somehow out of character. They are almost entirely male, and there are so many cars from out of state. Is Jack's really that great? Or could it be that other place further down the block, the Mansion House? And who is that strange man who always sits on their stoop at nights, like he owns the place? One evening, when Annabelle orders him off, he haughtily declares that he is the chief of police. Annabelle tells him she doesn't care who he is and chases him away. Chief of police, indeed! She's from New York! No one can fool her! Still, they are beginning to wonder if this place is as bucolic as they had thought.

Sunday mornings and trips to the Shiloh Baptist Church. Later, Pastor Allen makes a courtesy call to get acquainted with his new parishioners. He looks over the entire house, poking into every room, looking increasingly perplexed as he goes. Finally he says, "Well, this doesn't look like what they said it was."

"Oh?" inquires the mother. "What did they say?"

"I heard that a lady was moving up here with her three daughters and they were opening up a whore house.

I came to check it out for myself. I'm glad it's not true. Of course, I knew you weren't... I mean, it's obvious that this isn't... My, this is good cake." Frozen smiles all around. Reverend Allen makes a hasty departure.

Annabelle sits at the table holding her head in her hands. She is now sure her darkest suspicions are true. "Oh, my God, what have I done?" she moans. Has she made a horrible mistake? Did she uproot her family from a big-city Purgatory only to plant them in a small-town Hell? She looks around her, at the new house, her family's faces, the neighborhood. She thinks of their investment, her husband's job, her daughters' futures, the prostitutes in the houses around her. Slowly, the woman comes to the realization that there is only one thing they can do. They'll open a restaurant and cash in on some of this action.

346 Columbia Street, and the Chicken Shack is an instant success. Everyone helps out. Father built the tables, Mother and Sister-in-Law cook, the other siblings keep the books and wait on customers. Seventy-five people can be accommodated at the little wooden booths with the checked tablecloths and candles in the netted glass bowls. In the back is a small dance room, the latest tunes from the Hit Parade supplied by a juke box in the corner. The upstanding Baptists cheerfully serve red rice, potato salad, yams and fried chicken (but no alcohol) to madams, prostitutes, and their friends at prices everyone can live with. Aside from the lumberyard, the Chicken Shack is probably the first licit business to operate on the illicit block in years.

Columbia Street, three blocks from the River. In the decades before 1950 dozens of madams held sway in the little houses on what became known simply as "The Block." Dottie Pierson was at 342, Daisy Rawley at 358, Flo Whitney at 360, and Mae Healy at 328, "sponsored" by the brother of a local V.I.P. Lil Horton worked by appointment only, Bobbie Claire stabbed her boyfriend in a New Year's rage, and Carol Desmond moved into the place broken in by Kate Best, Saucy Nellie and later, Mrs. Ray Church. 1939 saw the arrival of Vera Faith, the attractive lady with the big wad of cash in her garter who became the unofficial spokeswoman of the Columbia Street madams. After World War II, Mrs. Faith ran an ad in the program of the Progressive Charity Ball of Poughkeepsie, New York. It read, "Vera's. Come on up, Boys. Sports merchandise."[2]

That said it all.

Columbia Street was famous as a well-managed, sensual shopping center, where even the most discriminating could find what they wanted. American servicemen at bases around the globe found their familiarity with The Block a common bond. A young college student, returning to his Hudson home by train was warned by the conductor, "You're going to Hudson, huh? Now you be careful up there, son." A man was driving a convertible with New York plates in Florida when hailed by another tourist.

"Where are you from?"

"Hudson, New York."

"What? That whore town?!"

For the uninitiated, any bartender or hotel employee could steer you towards whatever tickled your fancy. Taxi drivers acted as multi-talented tour guides, capable of writing numbers for gamblers and knowing where to find a drink, a crap game, and women of any description. They could even drive. Other people from various walks acted as "steerers" for The Block. The madams valued their service, and actively sought their favor and referrals. When a "steerer" deposited a customer at a madam's doorstep, his service would be noted, and on Fridays he would return to get his tip, fifty cents or a dollar a head.

Everyone knew that weekends were primarily for out-of-towners. The Block would be crowded with cars from Connecticut, Massachusetts, Vermont, and New Jersey, parked so thick it was tough to find a parking space. Men would come by train from New York or Albany to gamble at Dillon's or Mahota's, and then try to relieve a little tension with the girls, if they had any money left. Even the crew of a passing merchant ship was rumored to have deliberately sabotaged their vessel so they would be forced to stop at the little party town.

Legs Diamond kept at least one steady girlfriend on Columbia Street. When he went to get his haircut at Mike Finn's barbershop at 248 Warren, Mr. Finn would pull down all the shades, a sign to The Block that Mr. Diamond was in town and soon would be paying a visit. Featherweight boxing champion Willie Pep often made an appearance, and nearly 50 years later, movie star Robert Preston would fondly reminisce about his wild forays to Columbia Street, where presumably he was laying valuable groundwork for his future role in the "The Music Man."

During the War, President Roosevelt had come down hard on brothels operating near military installations, but without "regulated" sex, V.D. rates had soared.[3] Supervised places like Hudson provided a safer outlet, and servicemen on leave would come to The Block all the way from Sampson Air Force Base, over 50 miles away. In 1942, when an army division was briefly bivouacked nearby, the hormone level of the whole town rose.

The Hudson police kept a careful eye on unfamiliar men and automobiles. If they went to The Block, that was fine. But there was no mercy for out-of-towners causing trouble and bothering the "nice" local girls. Even those girls who weren't so nice could hope for the police to defend them. Still, there were flashers in the woods and parents angrily reporting their eight- or nine-year-old daughters being molested by strangers. The police invariably told them to "go see the judge."[4] Sometimes rowdy soldiers or college kids would get drunk and pick fights or vandalize porches and fences on Columbia Street. With 65 bars, often they just needed a jail cell to dry out in. The police logs had daily entries that read something like, "Officers Hart & Arkinson report they checked Columbia Street several times during their tour. Drove one Conn. car out of Block. Otherwise, quiet."[5]

Newcomers to Hudson frequently would get lost in the little town trying to find Diamond Street, which, unfortunately for them had been called Columbia Street since 1926. Carloads of men with out-of-state plates were constantly approaching children asking directions, apparently figuring that the little tykes wouldn't know what the men were up to. The tykes knew full well, but gave out the information with guileless smiles, enriching themselves with the nickel tips they'd receive in return. Indeed, the Fourth Street School overlooked The Block and when there was a fire in a bordello in the 1930's, the kids in the science lab rushed to the windows, gleefully picking out familiar faces among the johns jumping out the windows to escape the flames.

Some men wouldn't ask, but would just go up to likely looking places and try the doors. Residents of Third and Fourth Streets complained bitterly of their doorbells being rung at all hours, and the police were kept busy chasing would-be Romeos off innocent porches. Old Mrs. Benson in her towering, gloomy mansion at 306 Warren would become upset if her granddaughter tried to sit in the window. That was what the women did on Columbia Street, and Mrs. Benson didn't want strange men to get the wrong idea.

A young couple living on State near Fourth were giving a party one Saturday, when they noticed four unfamiliar men among their friends. After standing together for a minute, the group approached some of the female guests saying astoundingly rude things to them. The offended women complained to their hosts. When the husband demanded to know what the hell they were doing, the four looked confused and said, "Isn't this a whore house?" As they were being unceremoniously pitched out the door, the host noticed a red lantern hanging on the front porch. His wife later admitted she had put it there to identify the house for their friends. She had never heard the term "red light district." She just lived next to one.

Thursday was payday at many of the local mills and factories, and on that day the town was deluged with carloads of workers, out to sow their week's worth of wild oats. Some bosses would pack their laborers into trucks and send them to Columbia Street as a sort of fringe benefit. The boys from the Philmont mill would crank up their old Model T and careen into Hudson as soon as they got their pay envelopes. First, they'd stop off at one of the 65 bars and drink for a while. Then with testosterone levels fortified, someone would suggest that they "go put some coals on the fire." If they were lucky, the girls behind the shutters would advertise a sale. "Come on in, boys. Fifty cents off the price tonight." Capitalism at its finest. Afterwards, more drinking at Jack's or the Silver Dollar and some music on an accordion someone had brought along. Sometimes the boys would just go and sit in the Model T on Warren Street and try to pick up "regular" girls while avoiding the police. Why pay $1.50 when you can get it for free?

The locals knew that weeknights were really the best times for a visit, although the workers at the Thermo Mills on Front Street got paid Fridays at noon and some would mysteriously disappear from the afternoon shift. Once a week, one Hudson family followed a strange little ritual. Father, mother, and daughter would take a late afternoon walk, eventually bringing them past the corner of Columbia and Fourth. There the father would part company and proceed to his favorite bordello while his wife and child would go to a restaurant on Warren for tea. After 45 minutes or an hour, the husband would rejoin his family and they would walk home. During the week there wouldn't be a long wait, and not only would the girls be fresher, you could get your pick and maybe spend a little longer with your favorite. One enterprising lad convinced the madams to give a break to the "Hudson regulars": half price for him and his friends. Of course, being local wasn't always an advantage. Sons of the more well-known merchants or professional men were likely to hear,

"Do your parents know you're here? Go home, or I'll tell your father!" These boys went to Albany for fun.

Hudson provided something for everyone's tastes and pocketbooks. At the bottom of the line were Front Street establishments like Langlois Saloon, the Venice Bar, and the Curtis House, an old, rundown hotel on the corner of Allen, not actually on The Block, but related by business. Inside these shabby bars were a few desultory hookers waiting around to be picked up and taken to the rooms upstairs for two dollars or whatever they could get. The Curtis House also functioned as a "house of assignation," or a place where philandering couples could go, no questions asked. Close to the train station and boat landing, they catered heavily to the commuter crowd. Children were advised to hurry by on the opposite side of the street, as if they were full of white slavers. One time a relative of Paul Cocheran's was staying with him for a few days, and the man seemed afraid to go out and get a beer on his own. Apparently, on a previous visit to Hudson, the unsuspecting gentleman had wandered into the Venice Bar for a drink when a rather slovenly woman slithered up and point blank asked to be taken upstairs. Horrified, the poor man left his beer on the table and fled. "Are all the places like that here?" he asked. Mr. Cocheran was able to shepherd him to a less intimidating watering hole.

Then there was the optimistically named Mansion House at 332 Columbia Street. The biggest building on The Block, the Mansion House was three stories high, and boasted a large bar, tended by men with names like "Burger Baby" or "Woofing Sam." As the most flagrant place on The Block, strangers would come in to get information on action in the other houses, getting trapped by the Mansion House's own girls in the process. There were women of all sorts: big-breasted or boyish, large or delicate, blondes, brunettes, redheads, white, black, Asian—a woman for every taste and whim. On weekends there might be singers crooning love songs and smoky ballads to get the customers into the right mood. Some girls danced provocatively on the tables, while a dozen or so others slinked around in evening wear, looking to provide a good time for a fee. Mansion House girls were known for their tricks and versatility, and they kept a full stock of special toys on hand for those that liked to use them. The liquor served downstairs wasn't cheap, but the girls were very good at convincing their customers to buy round after round, all the while being attentive and flattering and making the men feel like a million dollars while they spent a similar sum. After a few drinks, the ladies' hands would roam to help the men's mood along, and that was usually enough to clinch the ticket to a half hour in heaven. Once, after a thirsty young fellow reached over and took a sip of his working-girlfriend's scotch, there ensued a torrent of cursing and insults. Storming out onto the street, he shouted, "I'll never come back here again! I'm paying a dollar a shot and she's drinking *tea!*"

A fire ended the Mansion House's reign in the 1940s, the volunteer firemen sent to fight the blaze getting involved in a personal rivalry and training the hoses on each other as the old building burned behind them. In later years, the shell was converted into a youth center where dancing on the tables was not allowed.

Evelyn White was every inch the lady. Her little house at 320 Columbia sat behind a tiny yard filled with beautiful flowers. She could often be seen, small and blonde, elegantly dressed and smelling of expensive perfume, driving around town in her impressive car, always attended by her two white poodles and sometimes by a handsome, younger man as well. Her girls were definitely of the first order, but for her especially exclusive clientele— those who demanded the utmost in discretion—Evelyn opened a private pleasure retreat in the hamlet of Hollowville, some 12 miles away. Only the most beautiful and accomplished women could work there, servicing the well-known politicians and celebrities.

The house in Hollowville was a large rambling structure with a wrap-around veranda, set in a lush green lawn with old trees, a barn, and a homemade memorial to the war dead, as much a gesture to the neighborhood as a paean to lost customers. Inside, the large rooms were furnished with fine antiques, the dining-room table always set with crystal and sterling, and the walls lined with velvet, providing a peculiarly sensual luxury. Upstairs, each bed, draped in satin, had a large "boudoir doll" sitting prominently on lace-covered pillows. A household staff served the guests, including a cook who would work out of two separate kitchens, one for the madam, and one for the girls. During the day, off-duty prostitutes would lounge on the porch reading and talking, dressed in shorts which seemed to scandalize the neighbors more than their nighttime activities. The local children were ordered to avoid Miss Evelyn's house like the plague, but they adored her and would rush over as soon as their parents' backs were turned. The lady always had sweets or candy ready for her young visitors, and at Christmas would have a huge dollhouse display set up just for them. When in Hudson, she always seemed to have a candy bar or lollipop in her purse for the boys and girls who flocked to her side. But Evelyn White could satisfy more than just a child's sweet tooth. A local clothing merchant had standing orders to supply clothes to any needy little ones he knew of, and send the bill to her. Another Evelyne the children knew, popular Hudson school teacher Evelyne West, sometimes would receive muffled phone calls inquiring about "private parties" and various illicit activities, but Mrs. West would always properly refer the callers to Miss White.

Once, during an election year, a prominent judge who had been one of Evelyn White's best customers, issued a warrant for her arrest on prostitution charges. The madam completely lost her ladylike composure at this betrayal, angrily storming around and venting to anyone within earshot, "That dirty S.O.B. gave me six months! Hell, when he got drunk in Hollowville and was running around naked waving a gun in the air, I was the one who took it out of his hand! If he had shot someone, his career would have been finished! I saved that bum's ass and look how he treats me!" Miss Evelyn's sentence was commuted on appeal. The judge lost his bid for re-election.

Mrs. Ray Church was an older lady who dressed like a spinster librarian but didn't always act like one. She operated out of both 323 and 325 Columbia, the same places where Kate Best and Saucy Nellie once proffered their services and George Best retired. Her house was furnished as she dressed, with a somewhat dull respectability, yet her sharp tongue and short temper made her unpopular with other madams. Perhaps Mrs. Church's bad humour was due to her "husband" Joe. Joe was tough, and didn't allow anyone to dispute the fact. He had a bar and pool hall further "upstreet," and if he felt some competitor had crossed him, he wasn't above going in and busting up the other man's place. He also wasn't above busting up Ray, stealing her money and jewelry whenever he saw fit. The Hudson police were well acquainted with Joe, but only Officer Thaddeus Raynor was deemed man enough to handle him. When Joe embarked on one of his rampages, Officer Raynor would be duly called out, and the two men would settle their differences on the street.

Big Minn and her daughter-in-law, Big Mae, were, well, big. Big Minn had a boyfriend named Doc and an extensive place, incorporating both 354 and 356 Columbia. Inside, one could find a six-foot, 300-pound madam, a bottomless box of chocolates, two chihuahuas, and seven or eight veteran prostitutes. Big Minn had a ready answer to those who accused her of keeping a "disorderly house." "I do not run a `Disorderly House'," she huffed, "I dust it every day and wash the windows." When she died in the late 1940s, there was a huge wake, followed by a sumptuous funeral and burial procession, replete with flower cars, limousines, and an enormous brass coffin. All of Minn's girls were in solemn attendance, dressed in suitable mourning and trying mightily not to look too ridiculous following in the garish parade as the townspeople sniggered from the sidelines. As soon as the show was over, Doc left town and the girls sought work elsewhere. They were heard to say that if anything ever happened to them, they wouldn't want all that fuss. Even in death, it would be too embarrassing.

Before the War there were a couple of black madams. Ma Brown had a little bar at 350, populated with girls you could take upstairs. And then there was the woman unfortunately known as "Nigger" Rose, who often could be found at the Mansion House. Mostly they had white girls working for them, but one could find black ones too. Black men, however, were rarely welcome. Newspapermen at the *Daily Star* knew the tastes of a prominent businessman who customarily drank with them at a nearby bar, so when he disappeared out the back door leading to the alley behind Columbia Street, they also knew exactly where he was heading.

"Where have you been?" they jeered when he returned some time later.

"Where have I been?" he answered. "Where have I been? You nosey old bastards, I'll tell you where I've been! I've been over in Columbia Street exploring the Darkest Depths of Africa, that's where I've been!"

For those who wanted diversions of a different sort, Esther Curtis provided a tall blonde called Foxy at her place at 322. Slender and good-looking, Foxy was different from the others and was usually found sitting quietly and fully dressed in a corner, instead of parading around in a negligee. However, Foxy could provide ecstasies that the other girls couldn't even dream of, ecstasies that drove some male customers wild. It seems that while Esther Curtis wore pants and walked like a man, Foxy *was* a man. And a very popular one, too.

One did not notice working girls (or boys) from The Block on Warren Street very often. Not only did they work all night and sleep all day, they tried hard to keep a low profile and in public were always well-mannered and modestly dressed. Frequently, the only way you could tell a fancy lady from a respectable one was that the fancy lady had nicer clothes. Hudson matrons would cross the street if they thought they saw one coming, while the men would stare at the ground, fervently hoping not be recognized. They had little to worry about, however, because the girls would never dream of embarrassing a client by hailing him on the street. That was bad for business, and besides, it was against the unwritten Code of Behavior.

Local merchants loved The Block, if only because its residents spent money like water and always bought the best. Sometimes shopkeepers would hike the prices for them: the well-dressed women with the big rolls of one dollar bills would pay anyway. Hymie Richmann of Richmann's Dress Shop basically lived off the Columbia Street trade. Occasionally the women would come to him, but usually he would be seen openly wheeling racks of expensive dresses and negligees down the street, making house calls to his valued female customers. The wags working at the *Daily Star* would shout out the back windows, "No dessert, Hymie!" while the dress salesman would chuckle all the way to the bank.

The hairdressers always did a brisk business. The girls never talked about their work, but it wasn't hard to figure out who they were. One beautiful regular would always come in with the same instructions, "Don't put a lot of goop on the back of my head. I spend a lot of time on my back." Madam Betty Belmont would order people around and not hesitate to tell anyone what she thought of him or her. Ragged and dirty women would turn up out of the blue and ask for "the works": manicure, pedicure, facial, hair set, and dye—lots of bleach. When they were finished, the strangers would pay and then shyly ask where Columbia Street was—hookers on a job interview.

The hairstylists always respected the girls' privacy and did what they could to keep them presentable, but other lady merchants were a little more squeamish. When "suspect" women would buy flowers from a certain shop on Warren, the lady proprietress would readily accept their dollar bills and then rush to the back room to wash her hands.

A teenaged boy working at a little grocery at the corner of Third and Columbia had a crush on the beautiful blonde who would come in almost daily, buying lots of Lux Soap, vinegar by the quart, and untold boxes of paper napkins. "Why does she buy so many napkins?" he asked the older boys. They just rolled their eyes, understanding how messy an activity sex could be. This lady was set up for business on her own in a small apartment, and the store's owner felt he was justified in taking some liberties. The boy blushed with embarrassment when the man grabbed her one day, but was gratified by her response. She slapped the man across the face and said, "I may work for a living, but I'm a customer and lady, and from now on you'll treat me like one!" The owner never touched her again.

Other tradesmen tried to maintain some kind of balance when dealing with Columbia Street. When Bart Delaney and his father sold ice cream from a cart, door to door, the boy would be sent into the houses to bring the women their orders and collect the money. "There's naked ladies in there!" he would shout as he ran back to his father. "Never mind what you see!" the man would bark. "Just deliver the ice cream and don't look!"[6] Other boys were frequently employed by the ladies to run errands like picking up sheets from the laundry, for which they would receive a dime or even a quarter. The older ones might be allowed to take their tips out "in trade." Contractors working on Columbia Street never had any trouble finding young assistants to accompany them on jobs. They just had trouble getting them to work.

One local electrician who frequently did legitimate contracting work at various locations on Columbia Street kept a special service truck with no lettering or advertising of any kind, in an attempt to maintain his reputation. Another handyman couldn't have cared less what anyone thought. He actively sought work at Mae Gordon's place at 352, where there was a blonde he was especially taken with. He put in a new line for the electric stove, installed a buzzer system, and rewired light fixtures, working there so often that he actually kept some tools in the house. One afternoon, when groping around in a dark bedroom for his toolbox, he found something other than his wire cutters. He had stumbled upon his sleeping beauty, and she just happened to be in the mood to offer free samples. All that vocational training had paid off after all.

Poor Al paid the price for his good manners. During one Christmas season, his men's store was full of "reputable" citizens when a flamboyant madam, shopping for presents for men-friends, swept into their midst with several employees in tow. After they spent a considerable amount of money, Al said, "It's a pleasure doing business with you ladies." The madam stopped in the middle of the store, and turning majestically like a battleship at sea, replied in a voice loud enough for Hudson gossips to hear for generations, "Well! It's a pleasure doing business with those who do business with us!"

In 1939, graduating high school senior, Miss Janice Silver, won Second Prize in an essay contest sponsored by the Chamber of Commerce. In her composition, entitled "Buy in Hudson," Miss Silver mused,

> Why should you support the citizens of your own town? Why should you establish the reputation of your city to be a thriving community? Why should you help to maintain those that aid you? These queries may be simply answered. If you buy in Hudson, the merchants prosper; they, in turn, benefit the city by engaging larger staffs. This is advantageous to all concerned... As citizens of Hudson, [the merchants] are responsible for the esteem with which Hudson is regarded by the remainder of the state. This opinion of non-residents is important, for, if someone desires to open a factory or a store, the financial condition of the town immediately presents itself, either as a magnet or an obstacle... To survive the competition of foreign cities, which is assuredly cutting the throat of Hudson business, apply the tourniquet of local trade to staunch the flowing blood of Hudson prosperity—Buy in Hudson![7]

Evidently, Miss Silver had her finger on the pulse of the community.

6: THE JOHNS, THE GIRLS, & THE MADAMS

❖

THE CARS CRUISE UP AND DOWN THE STREET, slowly, deliberately, with great purpose.[1] There are men walking in the shadows, singly and in groups, some open and boisterous, some lurking in the dark, trying not to draw attention to themselves. The old man stands furtively at the corner of Third and Columbia, looking up and down, up and down before he decides the coast is clear and he can scurry up the block to his clandestine rendezvous, just as he has done every few days for years. A group of high school boys giggles self-consciously as they consider the entreaties of the voices from the windows. The houses seem deserted, until upon closer inspection one notices the females whispering their advertising slogans, "Wanna make a baby?", "Wanna Trip

Around the World?" They sit behind closed shutters, almost invisible through the barely opened louvers. In colder weather, the shutters might be opened with the women posing like ribald Christmas toys on display behind frosty panes, urgent tapping drawing attention to the beckoning female opening her robe, displaying her goods. Customers might be able to get a glimpse of the parlour where the women await them, and in most of the houses, burning somewhere inside, is the time-honored symbol of the trade, a red light placed to be visible from the street. The roaming, hungry men make their selections and hurry up the walks into the little buildings. Mostly, they use the side or back doors, the proprietreses wishing to at least give the impression of protecting their clients' anonymity. A surreptitious rap and the madam admits them, sometimes via a buzzer system, unfamiliar faces eyed carefully as they make their approach.

The bawdy houses are fairly similar inside. Some are no more than flats, with a kitchen, living room, and a couple of tiny bedrooms all on one floor. Most occupy an entire house, but all contain the ubiquitous parlour where the men are received. There is very little that is special about them—no gilded chandeliers or spectacular furnishings or gaudy oil paintings of voluptuous females draped in impossible poses. Ray Church's place is typical. Her parlour has a carefully matched "living room set" from Berman's on Warren Street, a 9 x 12 rug with a vaguely Oriental pattern, an eight-day clock and a big Majestic radio against one wall, and a coal heater to provide warmth in the winter.[2] Some houses might have fancy wallpaper or elaborate bathroom fixtures, but there is little one can do to make a tired, working-class bungalow into Buckingham Palace. Of course, most of the men who come here aren't concentrating on interior decoration anyway. The lights are kept tantalizingly low, pink or amber lampshades showing off the women's complexions to their best advantage. It is "like walking into a seance," one customer says.

Here, potential clients wait, fidgeting, perhaps self-conscious or embarrassed. Groups of drunken buddies, long accustomed to whore-house ritual, loudly carry on and paw the women, making a showy display of their "manhood" to their friends. It can take on the mood of a dentist's office or that of a silent screen version of Sodom and Gomorrah, depending on the clientele of the moment. On especially busy evenings, the madams might handle the crowd by merely assigning the customers, particularly the new and inexperienced, to whatever prostitute is free. At other times, the chairs and sofas are occupied by the "inmates," three or four fancy ladies, dressed in their "come-on clothes."

You get treated well by these businesswomen. They are anxious to please, and try to make you feel welcome and important. They mingle freely, engaging in small talk and laughing at your jokes. They are usually dressed in silky robes or negligees, or sometimes in simple cotton housedresses, a few buttons or ties in front that can be quickly undone when their work commences. As you sit in your easy chair they glide over, fixing you with a smile and a greeting as they open their wraps, letting you inspect what they have to offer. Some of the women are knock-outs, some, more average. Many are very young, but it is not at all uncommon to find women over 40 among the rest.

You might notice other residents of the houses in the background. Local, usually black women, are on hand to clean and tend fires in the stoves, central heating being rare on Columbia Street. A whore house uses a lot of sheets and towels and a well-run place makes sure that each are put on fresh after every, well, almost every use. A pitcher of water and a bar of Lux Soap must be provided for each room, and of course, each sex-worker has to have her box of paper napkins standing at the ready by her work-station.

The customer makes a selection and is led to a tiny bedroom, a cubicle really, sometimes part of a larger room that has been divided with flimsy partitions. The light is much brighter here, coming perhaps from a single hanging fixture or a floor lamp. There is a bed, dresser, water pitcher in a china basin, and frequently, a doll or teddy bear, reminders of a distant, more innocent past. Sometimes there are no windows in this ad hoc sex-office, an electric fan providing some relief from summer's heat. Many girls keep a bottle of liquor or some beer under the bed and can offer you a quick drink for fifty cents or a dollar, another way to make a little money. The wall-mounted bottle-opener is in the hall, the glasses get washed in the bathroom sink.

Negotiations ensue. Each unmentionable act is carefully categorized and priced like on a menu in a roadside diner. In 1939 a Straight Party is $2.00; B.J., $2.00; Swallow, $2.50; Half & Half, $3.00; Trip Around the World, $3.50; kinky or unusual things, price on request. An all-night stay could be arranged for $15 or $20, a group party with more than one girl or customer for somewhat more, and the entire house could be taken for upwards of $300.

For short-term customers, drinks and bargaining finished, the procedure commences. The parties undress, the woman uses the pitcher and basin to carefully wash the man, taking particular care to inspect his privates for disease. Some foreplay is allowed, always leaving enough time for the agreed upon acts to be consummated before the 20 minutes is up. If it takes him more than a half hour, the girl or sometimes even the madam takes advantage of the very vulnerable moment to get him to finish or pay extra. The man sweats with exertion, his thoughts running wild, "Oh baby, baby! I'm in heaven! I'm Tarzan! I'm Superman!"

The woman whispers encouragement, her mind just as active, "..... I wonder what I should have for dinner? Oh, darn. I broke a nail." At last he "rings the gong" and the trip is over. The man dresses and pays, perhaps leaving a little extra in appreciation for a good time. After he leaves, she hides the money in a secret place, and then washes, making liberal use of vinegar and mouthwash, before dressing and returning to the parlour to start the cycle all over again.

The men are fairly ordinary. Workers, students, professionals of all ages out for a good time or a salve for their loneliness. A surprising number of them merely want to talk, expressing things that they couldn't say to their wives or girlfriends. Some are looking for instruction.

Joey is 16. An altar boy and student at St. Mary's Academy, his has been a good Irish-Catholic Hudson upbringing. As a toddler he had freely roamed the town on his tricycle, visiting all the shops up and down Warren, always under the watchful gaze of a friendly cop. When he was older, he picked cherries at a farm in Greenport, delivered hats from Mrs. Redmond's store, and dove in the River for coins that passengers would toss from the rail of the dayliner. It was a warm, safe childhood. But he remembered groups of pretty women going to his father's speakeasy, his mother hissing furiously in strangled whispers, "Don't you tell me they're good for business! I want them out of here!" He remembered the lady who smelled so nice who would always find him a piece of hard candy or a Hershey bar—but only, for some reason, when his mother wasn't looking.

Once when walking down Columbia Street after serving in church on Palm Sunday, a woman called him over to her window. She seemed to have just gotten out of bed, as she was only wearing a robe, but she wanted to know if the palms he was carrying were from church, and if so, could she have one? He fished a couple of palm fronds from the bunch, and she gave him a quarter. Odd. And then there were the times when his big brother would take him for afternoon rides in the family's touring car, only to stop on the same street and disappear for what seemed like an eternity. When he returned, he acted different, somehow. The boy never really understood what there was about this street that made people behave so strangely.

And then, puberty. Joey found himself fretting and unhappy, staring at girls he had known all his life in a whole new way. He listened to stories told by the boys on the basketball team, about celebrations held on The Block after every win... or loss... or practice. Desperately he wanted to go there too. One warm, summer night, he couldn't stand it any longer. His parents were out, and as Joey wandered restlessly around the house, he spied a couple of lonely-looking dollar bills peeking out of his father's bureau drawer. He paused for a moment, mindful of the dictum of the Church. Then he recalled a vision of that beautiful girl from school he saw that afternoon, her light, summer dress clinging ever so exquisitely to her.... He's out the door like a flash, the dollar bills clutched in his fist, Columbia Street and release looming large in his young mind's eye.

He has not gotten very far down The Block when a female voice breaks the silence. "Hey, Sweetie, looking for a good time?"

"Yeah!" he gushes, his Irish face lighting up with a broad smile of relief. "I sure am!" Quickly he hurries up the walk and the door unlocks with a click. The middle-aged madam studies him in the light.

"My! You're a young one!" she exclaims with a knowing smile. Joey has the fleeting fear that she might turn him away, but she ushers him to a seat in an overstuffed armchair about twice the size that he is, from where he surveys the scene. There are no women visible in the ordinary-looking living room, just a half-dozen or so men. He takes a closer look in the murky light and is startled to recognize one of his classmates from school, looking, if anything, more nervous than he is. It is all vaguely disappointing. Periodically, women in flimsy attire make appearances and the men cluster around. Joey continues to watch, holding his breath, when suddenly, he feels a tap on his shoulder. "You can go with her," the madam says.

Lost in a daze born of terror mixed with lust, the boy follows the girl through the curtains and up the stairs to a tiny, brightly lit little room. Turning to him, she asks bluntly what he wants to do. He is embarrassed because not only has he never spoken of sex in front of a woman before (let alone a naked one), he doesn't have the faintest idea what the choices are. They settle on a "straight party"—it's all he can afford—and she deftly gets down to work. She starts to wash him with the warm water, soap, and a sponge. The boy is in heaven, eyelids fluttering, imagining his passage into manhood, lusting for what he knows will happen after the sponge bath is over—those inviting arms, those luscious breasts, those quivering thighs, those...ooops. He's rung his gong. Not only is he more humiliated than he's ever been in his life, the girl makes him pay anyway. So much for romance.

Buddy has a special problem. His is a normal sexual appetite for a 21-year-old boy, but he has a certain physical defect that prevents him from following through on his desires. His steady girlfriend was willing enough, but ultimately even she wasn't able to help him, and they finally had to part in frustration. Buddy tries to console himself by visiting Columbia Street, hoping that the professionals there can cope with his deformity. At a well-known house one Thursday night, Buddy picks a girl. They go upstairs. Things seem to be proceeding normally. Suddenly the quiet is shattered by screaming. The girl rushes downstairs, stark naked, as the madam leaps up to see what the trouble is. "I won't do it!" cries the woman. "He'll kill me! He's going to kill me!" The madam is visibly upset by this commotion. She demands to know what is going on. "He's not sticking that thing in me!" the girl shrieks. "He'll rip me in two! He's just too big!" The madam, who has seen a lot in her life, greets this assertion with obvious skepticism.

"How big could he be?" she scoffs, looking at Buddy who stands forlornly in the background, wearing only his trousers hastily buttoned at the waist. The girl glares at him, as if requiring for him to answer. Blushing, the boy sheepishly unbuttons his pants and lets them fall to the floor.

The good madam stands rooted to the spot. Her jaw drops. She is transfixed by the vision before her eyes. Finally, not altering her gaze, she stirs herself into speech. "Honey," she stammers, "I've been dreaming about you all my life." And grabbing him by the hand, she drags the boy off to her own room. Buddy continues to see the woman on a regular basis until he goes off to war. Reportedly, he never has to pay.

Some boys at school love to tease a retarded classmate of theirs, gleefully exploiting his slowness and limited mental ability. One of them discovers that the boy's mother is a prostitute on The Block, and together, he and his friends conceive a diabolical plan. They will entice the lad, luring him to the very house where his mother works, and hopefully engineer an "accidental" meeting. They draw him aside and describe the joys of Columbia Street, doubling over with laughter at his clumsy enthusiasm to be included. They take him to The Block on a quiet evening, and wait for some action. The madam, having no idea who her drooling client is, simply assigns him to one of her less popular girls. The excited boy goes to the room indicated. The woman inside is naked and ready, not paying much attention as the customer starts to undress. It is not clear how far things progress before mother and son recognize each other, but he is soon seen rushing from the house, tears streaming down his red face, while his "friends" howl with laughter, delighted that their joke has worked so well.

*

Summer, 1934. Elizabeth is 14 years old and spending her vacation at her aunt's house on Staten Island. The young girl enjoys these forays to the edge of the Great City, and her home upstate seems very far away, indeed. She has a regular group of friends in her aunt's suburban neighborhood, but one day meets a new girl who seems different from the rest. She is somehow more sophisticated, more grown up. Her clothes are more expensive than the other girls' and she rides a brand-new bicycle with a big basket and a bell. She eyes Elizabeth, the little country bumpkin, and then challenges her without fanfare, the way young people do.

"Where are you from?" the girl demands.

"Philmont, upstate" answers Elizabeth.

"Philmont?" the girl ponders. "Is that near Hudson?"

"It's pretty close," Elizabeth allows.

"Have you ever heard of Columbia Street?" challenges the stranger.

"No," answers the 14-year-old truthfully.

"Well," says the girl, brightening with superiority, "My sister has a really good job on Columbia Street in Hudson. She bought me all this stuff. And she says that next year when I'm 16, she'll get me a job on Columbia Street, too."

The pecking order has been defined. The girls go off to play girlish games. But neither of them understands exactly what they have been talking about.

The female workers on Columbia Street did not usually come from Hudson itself. They were from New York, or Albany, or Connecticut, or Boston. One could find girls from Texas, and Arizona, and California. They would work for a while in Albany and then go over to Troy, then down to Hudson and perhaps on to New York City. Some madams kept houses in Troy or Albany in addition to Columbia Street, and would move their girls around from one to another, sending them in taxis supplied by one of Hudson's four taxi companies, earning them a fortune. Generally, the workers didn't stay in one place for much more than a month or two, as the customers wanted to see fresh faces and bodies. But occasionally, some popular prostitute would become a semi-permanent fixture, making her madam a lot of money.

The women would come to Columbia Street in many different ways. They might arrive on their own, wandering up Warren from the train station or boat dock, seeking out' the first beauty parlour they could find to have their hair done before heading to Columbia looking for a job. They might end up at the Mansion House, which often served as something like a prostitute's clearinghouse, the mother and son proprietors looking over the new arrivals and recommending them to various establishments in town. Many had friends already working in Hudson, who would refer them to their employers. Madams from other towns might call their colleagues with the name of a good worker they were sending over. Women from Columbia Street were occasionally sent down to New York or Albany to talk to the better quality street hookers in an attempt to recruit them to Hudson service. There were certain diners in Rensselaer and Albany where the owners would "collect" women, local madams paying a fee very much like buying slaves off the auction block. Pimps from Torrington, Connecticut or Pittsfield, Massachusetts would turn up with carloads of women, hoping to barter their talents in the Columbia Street marketplace. They would have complete control over their charges, returning to pick them up at the end of their stints and taking them elsewhere to sell. Many madams, however, preferred not to deal with pimps, loathe to share their workers' loyalties (or their own profits).

The girls' backgrounds were fairly similar, not having changed much since the days of Ellanora Kiere and Kate Best. They were not usually "wanton" or "fallen" women, but females who found themselves in a tight place without many choices. A great many were like Annie Spaulding, mere girls who had married too young and woke up too late. Some had young children to support when they suddenly found themselves widowed or abandoned. Some needed to escape a cruel husband or father. Many were ordinary girls who had "gotten into trouble," their families disowning them, equating their behavior with common prostitution, which ironically then became their only means of support. Some had an addiction to pay for. Some merely wanted independence. Some already had a job but just wanted extra cash. At least two were Syracuse University students, taking the four-hour train trip on weekends to work at Evelyn White's. One of them, charged with caring for her little brother, would merely bring him along, simply telling their unsuspecting parents that he was with her at work. Another girl from the Southwest truthfully told her customers, "If it was good enough for my mother, it's good enough for me." Very, very few were in it for the sex. Most, however, were in it for the money.

In 1941, a chemist with a bachelor's degree could make $1,400 working for a major corporation. A prostitute, just working weekends, could double that. A woman working full-time on Columbia Street could gross more than a doctor. Before the War, when opportunities for single women were few and pay was meager, those who were willing, able—and smart—could make a small fortune. As a local favorite named Vickie used to say, "I must have given away a million dollars' worth before I found out it was valuable."

When an unfamiliar girl turned up looking for a job, the madam would carefully check her references, making sure she was a professional and not addicted to drugs or alcohol. The girl's wardrobe would be inspected, right down to her underwear, to guarantee that the proper atmosphere would be maintained. The woman would then be required to strip and the madam would judge her cleanliness and check for any signs of disease. She would check any current health cards or send her to her own doctor for a blood test. And finally, the potential employee would be appraised by the madam's practiced eye, evaluating talent and enthusiasm for the job, for after all, service with a smile was essential to making a profit.

Those not accepted might try their luck at other houses, frequently finding a job on a Block with constant turnover. Some might accept a part-time position hanging around until a full-time place opened up. Those with pimps would be carted off to be offered to another establishment. For those who were too old, or ragged, or drug-addicted, or just plain unattractive, there was always the Curtis House or the Langlois Saloon across the street. And for those who couldn't even make it there, the dark alleys of Troy and Albany waited, where men weren't so picky, and the women could hide in the shadows.

For those who were accepted, whether full- or part-time, there was a life of hard work ahead of them, with lots of rules to learn. First of all, the madam and the client were always right, in that order. A girl could not refuse to go with a paying customer, and she could not take a customer unless he paid. Sexually, prostitutes were advised to "be ready for whatever they want and act like you've done it before," unless it was a case of sadistic or violent sex. (Madams didn't want their stock damaged.)

The madams also insisted that strict attention be paid to personal hygiene. There was no drinking on the job. Absolutely no drugs were allowed. Escape routes and hiding places had to be learned in case of a (very unlikely) raid. The girls were required to act like ladies on the rare occasions they were allowed to go out on their own, and not to draw attention to themselves by loose talk or trashy clothing. Soliciting on the streets was strictly forbidden. Seeing clients on the side was strictly forbidden. Having boyfriends on the side was strictly discouraged. Furthermore, the girls were charged a fee for room and board, personal laundry, the once-a-week doctor's visits, and sometimes even clothes if theirs were deemed inferior and the madam supplied something more appropriate, at a vastly inflated price, of course.

For full-timers, work was six or seven days a week, with one week off for the woman's "time of the month." Part-timers lived elsewhere and came in on weekends. The workday started at around five in the afternoon and lasted until the wee hours, but there were always early and late arrivals that had to be accommodated. New girls might be required to do "window duty," although eventually, everybody took a turn. Sometimes they would get into a bidding war with hookers in the other houses as they tried to lure confused customers to their door. "Don't go over there, honey. Those girls are all ugly. We've got what you want right here, and our prices are better..." When business was brisk, however, there was barely time to freshen up between johns, the madam sometimes having to pitch in herself. Each girl had a work-card that would be marked per client, so that the boss could keep track of what was owed her. Carol Desmond's girls used a heart-shaped hand punch, lending a little touch of Hallmark to her accounting system.

Once upstairs, the girls were expected to lobby hard for little "extras" to boost the price, teasing and enticing, reminding the client in seductive whispers what wonderful options came with this package. The prostitute was required to give the madam half her receipts, cheating being grounds for immediate dismissal, usually accompanied by torrents of abusive language. Although many girls kept the money in their rooms, some madams insisted upon collecting the cash between each session, divvying up the spoils at the end of the night. The most important rule of a whore house was, "Never get between a madam and her profit." Those girls with pimps then had to split what was left with them. Although the fees were standard, a professional might double or triple the price if she thought a client was green and she could get away with it. A good performance might garner a tip. "Regulars" might bring presents of jewelry or clothing. And, of course, pimps and madams didn't need to know about these little extras.

On the busiest nights, a girl might entertain three "tricks" per hour. Any more than that would deny the customers the 20 minutes they had paid for. On one Monday in 1949, Carol Desmond's heart-shaped punches indicated that Donna saw 20 men, Billie, 17, and Pat, 16. The next day, Donna saw 22 customers, Billie, 19, and Pat, 18.[3] Even with all the part-timers working, on a Saturday night it wasn't unheard of for a girl to see well over 30 panting clients, each one drawing increasingly on the woman's talents as an actress. The professional had to look at acting simply as a business skill, feigning ecstasy, doing whatever was necessary to bolster the fragile male ego, or simulating orgasm at the appropriate moment. Constant physical contact dulled her sensitivity, and many, if not most, viewed sex as a distasteful ordeal, tolerated only for the money. Once in a while, however, a girl might pick out someone special that she could enjoy and experience real orgasm.

During the day, the house girls would wander down to breakfast around noon. Sometimes there would be a cook. More often the women would shift for themselves. They would sit around the table over their coffee, gossiping about the johns from the night before. The afternoon would be taken up with hand laundry, doing nails, or going to the beauty parlour. They might read dime novels, play cards, or listen to the radio.

On nights during their "time of the month," the women might sit quietly by themselves in the parlour, their tiny bedrooms being used for business, while the madams would tactfully steer clients toward someone else. They might do a spell of window duty, or use these opportunities to go out to a movie or a bar like the Red Star Grill down by the Thermo Mills or Joe Robinson's place up on the Seventh Street Park. There the women would be given a table to themselves where they could relax. Off-duty, they were not meant to solicit, but, of course, no one could totally prevent male patrons from approaching them. When this happened the women would use the opportunity to hand over a business card.

Working women could also get out if some local V.I.P. wanted to pay for their time and escort them to some "hot spot" for dinner and dancing in a town where they weren't known. Even though it was strictly against house rules for a worker to date a client, the madams were capable of stretching a point in the case of a client with the power to put them in jail.[4]

Most of the men treated the women as well as can be expected, but there were those who proved to be a problem. Despite the madams' best efforts, there was occasional violence as someone with a little too much drink or a little too much ego would take out his frustrations on the woman in his control. Other customers or the Hudson police might be called upon to break up fights or rescue a worker in trouble. Many of the madams had men in residence who could handle unruly guests. Still, a girl was shot and killed at Ray Church's house in the 1930s and there were other assaults, including one madam who stabbed a man who had gotten out of hand.

Usually, the indignities the women had to face were of a less physical, but perhaps more cruel nature. Sometimes they could retaliate. One morning in the 1940s, a prostitute, dressed only in a negligee, was confronted by two men doing repair work in her house. One of them stopped her and tried to open her robe, but she was definitely off-duty. "I get paid for this!" she snapped in an attempt to maintain her dignity. In response, he grabbed her again, forcibly ripping open her clothes and spitting on her nakedness. "There! That's what I think of that!" he shouted, the two convulsing in raucous laughter at the hilarious insult, while the woman fumed in silence.

A couple of weeks later, dressed in a respectable suit and hat, the lady was in the waiting room of a local doctor's office for her weekly checkup. The room was full of matrons and their children, as well as one of the repairmen. With everyone watching, the prostitute walked directly up to him and addressed him by name (strictly against the rules). She proceeded to converse familiarly, the man blushing and seeking an avenue of escape, when she went in for the kill.

"You know, I'm here because I've got some kind of cyst on my tit," she said, adding, "Wanna see?" at which point she opened her blouse and hauled out the member in question. The matrons squealed and hid their children's eyes, the man growing visibly smaller by the minute. After the prostitute finished with the doctor, the man was still there, shuddering under the condemning gaze of Respectable Hudson. But, the lady wasn't finished. "Oh, drive me home, won't you, sweetie? I'm tired, and you know where I live." The man, totally humiliated, rushed her out the door and into his car—anything to get away from those mothers' stares. The woman smiled at what she had done to the fellow's reputation as the car pulled away from the curb. The whore house was all of two blocks away.

It may be hard to believe that a hardened prostitute could fall in love with a client, but it sometimes happened. A certain touch, a word, an act of humanity might be enough to cause a lonely woman to cross the line. It was fairly common to see a smitten working girl supporting some waste of a boyfriend, setting him up in a room or apartment, buying him expensive presents at Kritzman's or Marsh's. Occasionally, Hudson residents would discover these tainted boarders, their suspicions aroused by a handsome man sitting around all day, doing nothing, while his "wife" would disappear late in the afternoon and not return until dawn. One prostitute who fell for a local guy showered him with presents and trinkets, eagerly awaiting his regular trips to her house. As was inevitable he tired of her, and one night made a big show of bypassing his "steady" to escort one of her co-workers upstairs. It was his way to signal the end of their "relationship." She was crushed. He kept all the presents.

Some men had favorites and returned night after night. They thought they were in love, but were usually mistaken. If their darling was occupied when they arrived, they pouted and muttered, looking darkly at each departing guest, wondering if he was the one who had usurped his beloved's attentions.

Some got married, usually with disastrous results. Those who could never forget their wives' pasts were disabled with jealousy and suspicions. Henry, married to a sex-worker, was kept awake night after night by her endless sobbing. She seemed heartbroken, and he couldn't imagine what he'd done wrong. He was amazed by the truth. She wept for her former pimp, electrocuted by the State for murdering one of his girls. She wept for her lost independence and the men vying for her attentions. After the divorce, she returned to her old job on The Block.

Infatuations with the customers could breed jealousies and friction in a whore house. Nasty fights might erupt if one worker thought another was out to steal her "beau." Occasionally, lesbian relationships would develop, women seeking solace from each other, and generating new kinds of rivalries to deal with. The women might also resent a co-worker if she seemed to be too popular, grabbing the lion's share of the profits and attention. However, the prostitutes usually got on well together, united by a common bond and destined to move on fairly soon anyway. They actually tended to be a softhearted lot, always ready to listen to another's troubles, sometimes banding together to help out with money when a colleague was faced with one of the "dilemmas of the trade."

Venereal disease was something of which everyone was justifiably terrified. Even though a weekly check by a doctor became required in Hudson during the 1930s, true professionals were getting checked long before that as a matter of course. Prostitutes working before 1910 had no recourse but luck and home remedies if they got infected, untreated venereal diseases causing infertility, blindness, painful bone disorders, and insanity, while continuing to gnaw away at a person's insides, leading ultimately to death. Although condoms existed, it was unthinkable to expect a man to wear one in a bordello, and a woman's defense was limited to the meticulous inspection of her partner before contact occurred. If a girl got V.D., the madam would usually blame her for not checking properly, and then fire her and see that she was blacklisted, there being very little else that could be done. Just before World War I, Paul Ehrlich of Germany developed the first cure for syphilis, requiring regular therapy with arsenic or mercury. Although it could clear up the infection, it also could take years, making the patient sick and weak with convulsions and vomiting, if it didn't kill her in the process. It was very expensive besides, most common prostitutes not having the resources to take advantage of the treatment. Gonorrhea could sometimes be treated in men by incorporating a very long and complicated process, but about all that could be done for women was surgery to relieve some of the excruciating build-up of pus in her sexual organs, which did nothing but delay the inevitable.[5] Finally in 1945, penicillin became available to the general public, and for a few decades at least, sexually transmitted diseases seemed vanquished.

Pregnancy was as hard to avoid as venereal disease for the working woman. Since condoms were not an option, the women used whatever other birth-control devices were available to them, such as vaginal sponges or jellies. They could try using the "rhythm method," but that was not always practical for someone having sex with three or four hundred men a month. Most long-term professionals experienced a pregnancy sometime in their careers, which left them two choices: have the baby or seek an illegal abortion.

Every madam had a list of local abortionists. Most were out-of-town doctors, but there were also midwives, dentists, or nurses who could be found to perform the operation. Some girls would make the trip to Albany or New York, but for those seeking to save money, their fellow workers would pitch in to help them out. There were various homemade remedies and purgatives that were supposed to induce spontaneous miscarriages, but when they failed there was always someone with some wire, a long hat pin, or some other horrible instrument. All too often, the abortion would spell an emergency trip to a local physician, if not death.

For a woman who chose to have her child, a maternity leave would be granted when she started to show. Hopefully, she would have saved enough money to carry her through her confinement, but if not, she would have to depend on family or try to get some kind of regular job. Once the baby was born, mother and child would face an enforced separation as there was simply no place in a whore house for a baby to live. The prostitutes and madams tended to be sentimental towards children, and there were plenty more women than Evelyn White who would shower the little ones with candy and nickels. Occasionally, a child would take up residence in a Columbia Street house for some reason, swing sets and wading pools magically appearing in back yards up and down The Block as the women competed for the toddler's affections. Some were known to bring a nursing newborn to live with them at work, hiring a babysitter to care for the child in the attic or kitchen while the mother earned her living. These arrangements, however, could never last for long.

Of course, many women had children already when they entered the business. Some were left with relatives or ex-husbands. Many children boarded with strangers in Albany or Troy, their mothers rushing to see them during their time off. Some were raised in ignorance of their mothers' lives, others eventually stepped into their mothers' shoes.

There was an older prostitute who often could be found at Clyde's Restaurant in Claverack during her free time. She was attractive and refined, sitting by herself, drinking dainty, ladies' drinks. Her adolescent daughter lived in New York, and knew only that her mother had a great job in Hudson, making lots of money. One day, the daughter contrived to give the mother a treat, paying a surprise visit to the address she had off her mother's letters. The mother was more horrified than surprised, and the daughter was devastated. She fled the scene in panic, and all the mother could do was watch her leave. Later she was back in Clyde's, awash in tears and alcohol. Shoving nickels into the jukebox, she played the same tune over and over. "That's me," she sobbed to anyone who came near, "I'm just a melancholy baby."

Holidays like Christmas and Thanksgiving were the hardest on the girls. Business dropped off dramatically as the men stayed home with their families, and the women found themselves with plenty of time to ponder their loneliness. Certainly, some would have a child left somewhere or parents and siblings who still welcomed them, but the holidays found Columbia Street full of women with no place to go. The madams tried to make life a little festive. There would be gifts and decorations. Evelyn White gave her famous party, and one Columbia Street house had a Christmas tree so elaborate that young Mr. Neefus, the photographer, was hired to record it on film. Many women would attend services at one of Hudson's 20 churches, and then come home and just drink. In a few weeks they would be off to another place, another boss, another crowd of faceless males. If syphilis, a botched abortion, or the bottle didn't get them, time would. The professional prostitute rarely lasted more than seven or eight years.

For many, the end of their working lives, totally dominated by johns, pimps, and madams, would find them broken in purse and spirit, with few options to fall back on. The lucky ones would find some security in family or friends, slowly distancing themselves from Columbia Street. Others would disappear into a grubby world of rented rooms and menial jobs, waxing nostalgic for their lost youth when men lined up to pay $2.00 for a moment of love. One might see them, haunting the bars, drunkenly carrying on about their days as Queens of The Block. As time went on, the men miraculously grew more handsome, the fees more spectacular. Even then, they might have a low-life boyfriend or even turn an occasional trick for two dollars or the price of a drink, never truly able to grow out of their past.

Of course, many working women never intended to stay at it very long. They merely continued until they found something better, saving their money to buy a business or go to school. Some managed to get happily married and raise a successful family. Years later they fit seamlessly into their middle-class neighborhoods, their secret former careers no more important than some nearly forgotten summer job.

And then there were always a few who graduated into madamhood.

*

The letters tell her story. Mae was different from most of the other madams on The Block in that she actually grew up in Hudson. Her grandparents were neighbors of Ellanora Kiere, witnessing the shooting of Charley Hermance during that snowy Christmas season so many years before. In 1906, her parents took a lease on the house that would eventually become Mae's bordello, a crude "X" signifying Mae's mother's agreement to pay $8.00 a month for the wooden, two-story structure. Most of her life was spent among the bootleggers and prostitutes on the wrong side of Warren Street, such as Arthur Trebilcox who hired women to dance the St. Louis, and Miss Isabel who hired women for more private performances. The brown-haired, blue-eyed girl grew up quickly, not exactly a beauty, but with a full figure that made her seem older than she was. As soon as she turned 14 she was sent to work in one of Hudson's factories, apparently leaving school to do so. At 15 she was already granting favors to lonely sailors visiting The Block, receiving sappy love letters from various American military bases around the world.

An early liaison produced a daughter, but Mae still sought to indulge her passion for pretty clothes and fast men. Before long she seemed to be working in the houses of Troy, Albany, and even Hudson, using a variety of aliases and saving her money. She euphemistically referred to her new profession as working in a "beauty parlour."

When Mae was around 30, she seems to have begun thinking about starting her own operation. Working out of

Albany, she sought out an old colleague in New Haven who wrote back to her:

> Mae, if you think we could make any money on the Street it will be O.K. with me. But I don't think I would care about going to Hudson because I never know who will come in there. If things are any good on the Street, write and let me know and I will come up. Say about 100 or so a week it would pay to come up there. So write and let me know and if so I will come right up...[6]

Once word got out that Mae was hiring, many women started applying for a job. Friends would ask her to hire acquaintances on the lam. Scribbled notes would request interviews at various locations around Albany.

If Mae had been like Ellanora Kiere, Kate Best, and other budding madams, there would have been a man somewhere in the background, footing the start-up costs (and taking most of the profits). But like others who began completely independently, Mae was careful with her money. She bought everything "on time:" bedding at Berman's, housewares at Macy's Dry Goods, furniture at Kestenbaum & Weinstein's on Warren Street, where she paid off her bill at the rate of $2 or $3 a week—for four years. Moving in with her mother in the old house on Columbia Street, she soon assembled a "stable" of three or four girls in decidedly low-rent surroundings. Her employees were renowned for their beauty, with perfect hair and skin, and flawless figures, but Mae's house was not necessarily considered the best place to work, as one man wrote to his working girlfriend:

> I remember the last time you was there.
> You said what a place. No bath tub or lights.
> But now you don't mind that. And another
> thing. You say it's getting too hot to stay there.
> Is that why you are going to leave?[7]

In the winters, Mae depended on coal and body heat to keep her customers warm...

> Boy, I got a pip of a cold down there
> Saturday night. When you sleep in that house,
> the only thing to bring is your sheep-lined
> sheets, mommy... So, you don't like it there.
> Well, I can't blame you. No lights and no bath
> tub... [8]

...while her employees depended on hot gossip:

> Say, sugar, don't be telling those girls what
> love letters I write. I don't like it. You know
> how it is. You don't have to tell people. They're
> not interested bout our love affair. You know,
> sugar, things are not like they suppose to
> be...but as long as you keep [your] nose clean, I
> don't mine it a lot...[9]

Meanwhile, Mae was socking away her profits, maintaining accounts in several banks in Hudson as well as Albany where she had opened another bordello. By 1949, Columbia Street madams were making between $20,000 and $30,000 a year, tax-free, while a Hudson cop made about $2,000.[10] Mae bought a big Durant sedan, equipped with a deluxe 6-tube Superheterodyne Emerson radio, doused herself with Mae West "Parfum" ("Fascinating, Romantic, and Alluring"), and wore a luxurious fur coat from M. Solomon of Albany—paid for in installments, of course. Once she was even sued for nonpayment for an item bought on "short credit." The amount in question: $34.37.[11] And when she started getting her Columbia Street house ready for business in the 1930s, she received an irate note:

> Dear Madam,
>
> I see that you are having your house all fixed up. You have made lots of excuses about paying me the $16 dollars due. Now I have waited as long as I intend to... I will wait only until Monday next and if I don't hear from you by that time I certainly will summons you to Court...[12]

Mae was also something of a hypochondriac, constantly complaining to friends and family of aches and pains, her medicine cabinet full of mail-order remedies. Her formerly full figure had grown into gigantic proportions, not helping her angina or asthma. She sent away for Dr. Van Valkenburg's special diet and Edna Wallace Hopper's "White Youth Pack" to clear up blackheads and take "Ten Years off your Face in Ten Minutes." Humphrey's Formula "99" was for constipation and Pixine Ointment for rashes. Every letter has her in bed with a cold, or the flu, or hay fever, her supposedly rotten health becoming a favorite topic of conversation. As for Mae's face and figure, it was probably a good thing that she was the boss and not a worker.

With thousands in the bank, Mae could afford to be generous. But still her daughter constantly wrote pathetic letters begging for money and attention. The daughter had been raised in Albany, being perhaps 14 when her mother opened the business in Hudson. She seems to have followed in her mother's footsteps, at least as far as men were concerned. A prepubescent love letter— "Gee, but I will be lonely without you, honey..." —not only gives "best regards to your mother," but also to all of the other hookers working with her at the time, by name. Neither the author nor recipient could have been more than 11 years old.[13] More mature missives from a parade of sailors and other admirers follow. There is an early marriage gone bad, then an affair with a married man, another marriage, and then a baby. Mae's career has been hard on her child, who has grown up seeking affection wherever she can find it.

> Dear Mother,
>
> I still haven't heard from you, although you took time to write to P. What does it mean anyway? Don't you care what happens to me? It seems that way... If you could send me some money it would be swell & don't worry. It wouldn't be used for drinking cause that's a small thing to me now. I don't care if I never have a drink. Well there's no news here so I guess this is about all. Only I still can't understand why you didn't write...[14]

Mae's daughter merely reflected the pressures of being raised as a virtual fugitive. Madams, like their employees, were unable to give their children the attention they deserved. Vera Faith boarded her daughter with a Polish couple right in Hudson, paying the boy who delivered her groceries to escort the girl to the movies and to

McKinistry's Drug Store for a soda afterwards. One madam's daughter was kept so secret that when the young woman eventually applied for a social security number, she found there was no record of her birth. Officially, she didn't exist.

But then, these women didn't really have time to be Andy Hardy-type mothers. Like any other business owners, they had a host of things to worry about in addition to their children. There were one or more houses to maintain, women to feed, customers to satisfy. For most of her years on The Block, Mae had to deal with coal stoves, gas lights, and kerosene lamps, The Block not becoming totally electrified until 1949. A fire destroyed her garage along with her Durant sedan, so she bought a nice Plymouth—secondhand, of course. A madam seemingly had to be everywhere at once working simultaneously as a retailer and a psychologist. Her girls were young, many of them lonely and from broken homes, and Mae would often dispense advice or lend her big shoulder to cry on. Indeed, she gained a reputation for being an almost stereotypically big-hearted (if not big-spending) madam. "After all, Mae, you know you have been just like a Mother to me and I'm not forgetting it..."[15] One madam rented a cottage at nearby Lake Taghkanic, purely as a place for her girls to get a little R & R. Happy hookers meant happy clients.

Regular customers also had to be accommodated, and Columbia Street madams kept careful records of the men's sexual quirks and preferences in notebooks for easy reference. For instance, there was the guy who could not get aroused if there was anyone touching him or even visible. He would always repair, stark naked, to the back yard, a soft piece of hemp wrapped around his privates and attached to a long cord which ran through a window, allowing an unseen girl to manipulate his organ from inside the house with little, rhythmic tugs. This arrangement lasted until one winter night, when the designated prostitute got involved in an argument with another girl and completely forgot about the naked man standing in the snow with a string tied to his penis. He very nearly froze to death.

Another regular required a coffin-like box to be kept against his arrival. Concealed behind a curtain, the guest would lie in the box, wrapped in a cape, feigning death. After a suitable interval, a naked prostitute would be sent behind the drape. The man would sit up, the girl would scream and scream on cue—and that was all that was needed for him to ring his gong. Mae got a lot of money for that one.

She also had to keep an eye on her guests to weed out troublemakers. Drunks were turned away at the door. Groups of students could be loud and rarely had much money. They also had a nasty habit of stealing the girls' underthings or little knick-knacks as mementos or perhaps trophies to be brandished in a locker room. There were rowdies who would vandalize porches, rip shutters off their hinges, or try to break down the door after she had locked them out. Servicemen could tear a house apart if they weren't watched carefully, and someone was always having to chase away adolescent boys and others who would be caught peeking through the bedroom windows with their pants down around their ankles. Also, everyone knew that a lot of cash was kept in a whore house, and residents had to guard against armed men robbing the place, sometimes with the aid of one of the girls. In 1947, one of Mae's most dependable female employees stole $5,000 and fled West. No one could be trusted.[16]

To take care of some of the more violent customers, the police were always around, safeguarding Hudson's most valuable assets, but many madams also kept men for security. Mrs. Ray Church had Joe. Ma Brown had the appropriately named "Big Charlie." Big Minn kept Doc Van Aken, and Mae Healy had the infamous Dutch Hoodmacher, renowned for his stamina when being entertained by the ladies, and known to carry a baby photograph, supposedly of himself, doctored to have certain male parts enlarged to generous adult size.

Mae usually had a man living somewhere in her house, but her booming voice and huge dimensions were intimidating enough. As with most madams, she had a second-in-command to take over when she was away in Albany visiting her daughter, recruiting new help, or tending to her house there. This woman normally worked as a prostitute, but would collect the money and keep the accounts in the boss's absence, to be gone over with a fine-toothed comb upon her return. Mae's bookkeeping had to encompass the girls' earnings, their fees for room, board, and laundry, cleaning help, outlays to the taxi drivers, waiters, and others who steered clients to her place—and bribes.

A madam had rules to follow as well. She had to keep her girls in line, keep her house free from disease, and had to cooperate with the authorities, which could mean anything from supplying V.I.P.s with dates to paying for protection. Breaking the rules could mean getting raided and fined or even run out of town. Raids were very infrequent, one house in 1936, two in 1941, one in 1949 where police arrested the 65-year-old madam hiding in the bushes and two of her girls cowering on the floor of a taxi waiting at the curb. But then, that was a new operation, the madam an Italian from New York, and people were suspicious of outsiders.

Mae herself was arrested in 1949, but the charges were eventually dropped.[17] She supposed that someone was just trying to make a point. If any girls got arrested in a raid, the madams would immediately go and pay their fines (just about the only thing they regularly did pay for) and bring them home. Of course, sometimes a complaint or a crusader would compel the Hudson police to try a raid as a matter of form, but that was always easily taken care of. When the officer approached the front door, the window girls would know to activate the electric door locks. The policeman would try the door, and unable to open it, would go away, making no other attempt to enter. That way he could report that he had made an investigation, but found no illegal activity.[18] When they were making friendlier visits, they would come around to the back. Still, everyone remembered the time early in 1939 when almost all the madams in Hudson were quietly arrested and fined, some up to $500.[19] Of course it was a purely political move and business didn't even skip a beat, but it served as a reminder that Columbia Street flourished only at the discretion of the powers that be. But then, even these powers couldn't always agree. Once during the 1940s, two local politicians, each of whom "sponsored" a house, got into a feud and threatened to have each other's place shut down. Nothing came of it.

Every week, Mae made up envelopes filled with cash, various people's initials written on the outside.[20] Her ledger contained meticulous entries for coal and milk, as well as lists of the nicknames of local men in authority with dollar amounts—"$5" or "$10"—written next to them. Everyone seemed to get something, and cops on the beat often didn't even have to ask; money was just thrust through the louvers of the shutters as they walked down the street. On other occasions, they'd come to the door, and Mae's paperboy breathlessly told his friends of being forced to hide in a kitchen cupboard as a man in uniform arrived for his bribe. However, when some officials in town started getting greedy, demanding more money and things like "porterhouse steaks topped off with Schrafft's chocolates,"[21] the madams decided to take some action: In 1949, a delegation of three, dressed in their best and led by Vera Faith, paid a call on the police commissioner to ask that the pay-offs be reduced. They were tired of giving $5.00 or $10.00 to anyone who came along, and they wanted the commissioner to fix a flat fee that would be paid to one person in charge, and then distributed by him. After all, increased overhead just meant passing on the cost to the consumers, who, by 1949 were already paying $6.00 for a straight party, and at that rate, how could Hudson compete with Troy? The commissioner expressed horrified indignation and "chased them out."[22] The Block limped on.

By 1949, however, Columbia Street was in obvious decline. The Mansion House was gone, as was the Curtis House. Ray Church, Big Minn, and Dottie Pierson were all dead, and others had retired. There seemed to be fewer houses operating than there had been in years. Whereas in

1939, 50 to 75 women might have been working on Columbia Street, now the number was closer to 30, if that, and rowdy kids from out of town made it necessary to close as early as eight o'clock on some nights.

Mae and others were also finding that it was getting harder to recruit workers. For one thing, the introduction of welfare and unemployment insurance meant that poor young women desperate to support their babies had financial assistance. But something else had gradually changed: Not only did women during the War discover that they could earn decent money working at jobs once held by men, men discovered that it wasn't always necessary to pay a woman to sleep with them. Ordinary women were beginning to express their independence, and the madams of Columbia Street could only observe this evidence of moral decay and shake their heads.

Even though there were fewer houses operating, there was no shortage of business, and Hudson still lived up to its long-standing reputation as the Sin Capital of the East. Gambling was bigger than ever, and the famous floating crap game attracted people from all over. Senator Estes Kefauver started his highly publicized nationwide campaign against organized vice, and New York's Governor Dewey was embarrassed when one of his chief advisors was caught in a New York City sting. Soon, he was seeking ways to head off a political scandal, and rumblings could be felt on Columbia Street. The American Social Hygiene Association sent undercover investigators to The Block as part of their nationwide survey of vice. A prostitute told one of them that she'd heard that it wouldn't be long before there would be a big crack-down.[23] The Association rated Hudson as "bad."[24] Madams and their girls started noticing nervous-looking men hanging out on the street wearing gray socks. Only State Troopers wore gray socks. All the girls and their friends knew something was up:

> I'd have left Sunday when I heard the F.B.I. men were there. While I'm writing about F.B.I., tear up the letters because if they find them they might look me up and cause lots of trouble...[25]

Mae received a warning from a friend in Albany:

> Since you went away, thing or all closed here. Policy & Clearing House, and Pool Romes. i earnestly hope you'll keep out of trouble as a 500.00 fine is some fine. Hardly worth taking a chance for the little you do down there, but as you say what are you going to do with a help less crowed such as you have... sorry to hear you are confiend to your bed a with a cold...[26]

Mae's friend couldn't spell, but she sure gave good advice.

7: THE END

J UNE 23, 1950, AND THE BIG STORY IN THE LOCAL papers is the upcoming Soap Box Derby. Young Craig Thorn has been chosen to organize the race down the hill on upper Columbia Street by the hospital, and local merchants are busily sponsoring area youngsters in the construction of their cars. Out near Chicago, over 50 people have been killed in the nation's worst airline disaster ever. The ultra-modern New Jersey Turnpike is nearing completion, and the start of the Korean War is two short days away—an editorial in the *Daily Star* has called for bomb shelters to be built in the city's schools, with atomic-proof buildings to be erected later. But all this seems distant as the weekend gets under way.[1]

It is a typical Friday night in the old river town. Charlie Beecher has hired some professional wrestlers to put on a

match in the ring he has built behind his restaurant at
Second and Columbia. His customers order more beer
and sandwiches as they place bets among themselves on
the outcome of the contest. In a building down the block,
seven men commence a game of chance. Uptown, the
bars and brothels are doing a brisk business. Mark, one
of Mae Gordon's "steerers," is on his way up Columbia
Street to collect his tips for the johns he has sent to her
house this week. These days he's getting a dollar a head.
Mae Healy sits at her kitchen table with a group of men,
pouring coffee and opening the steamed clams that have
just been delivered, while her girls take care of the
clients gathered in the parlour. The Chicken Shack has
closed for the day, the family that runs it listening to the
radio in their living room upstairs. At his home in
Claverack, District Attorney John N. McLaren fidgets
nervously as he tries to relax. He worries about some
recent actions he has taken and walks around like a man
lately condemned to the gallows. Meanwhile, John J.
Sullivan sits happily at his home with Mrs. Sullivan,
enjoying the company of his family. This has been a
satisfying week for him. Wednesday marked his first day
on the job as Chief of the Hudson Police Department and
tomorrow he celebrates his 25th wedding anniversary.
Life, he reflects, is good.

Life has its challenges, however. A couple of men
driving north on Fairview Avenue pass a motorcade of
trucks and plain Ford sedans heading south into town.
Sensing something momentous, the pair turn around and
follow the procession back to Hudson. A teenaged girl is
drawn to her window by the sound of motors. Truck after
truck is heading up Third Street, like some anonymous

military convoy. Mark, Mae Gordon's steerer, slows his pace as he sees a line of cars and trucks draw up, blocking the intersection of Columbia and Third. Evening strollers wonder what the trouble is as they notice a group of people sprint to the entrance of the dark store at 7 South Front. Some men in uniform ring Chief Sullivan's doorbell and ask the startled man to accompany them for a ride. A few minutes later, Desk Sergeant Fred Finck is amazed to look up and see the uniformed group, with the chief in tow, march into the police station and block all the exits, the stern faces under their broad-brimmed hats telling the Hudson police officers on duty that they aren't going anywhere for awhile. In Claverack, District Attorney McLaren receives a telephone call. "The raid has started," a voice tells him.

Chief Inspector McGarvey of the New York State Police, Troop G, Troy, has meticulously briefed his men on what they are to do. Most of them did not know until an hour or so before exactly what their mission was, but now they are ready, armed with nightsticks, sledgehammers, and crow bars, wristwatches perfectly synchronized. Inspector McGarvey has assigned the targets: 322, 325, 328, 340, 344, 352. The cars mass at the ends of The Block and at the signal, swoop into their places in front of the unsuspecting houses. Swiftly the troopers leave the vehicles and arrange themselves at all the entrances, three in front, three in back, three on the sides, wherever a man or a woman could attempt to escape. Seeing their approach, some of the window girls activate the electric doorlocks, but tonight that is not going to make a difference. The troopers stand poised on the stoops, staring intently at their watches, ready to strike together at precisely the same moment. As fifty second-hands sweep by eleven o'clock p.m., the attack begins.

There is a noise, loud and sharp, like a clap of thunder as the troopers bring their sledgehammers down on the whore-house doors in one, unified motion. The family at the Chicken Shack, thinking there has been an explosion, rushes to the windows. The girls want to go outside, but their father wisely forbids it. For up and down the 300-block of Columbia Street there is pure pandemonium. Ordinary residents pour out of their houses to see the state troopers splintering brothel doors with their axes and crow bars. There is the sound of shattering glass as half-naked men and women crash through windows and hurl themselves into the shrubbery, desperately trying to escape. The troopers remaining outside scatter in every direction, attempting to catch the fleeing hookers and johns before they can get away. Mark, the steerer, turns in his tracks as he watches the siege taking place at Mae Gordon's. He realizes that the best place for him at this moment is home in bed, with the covers pulled far over head.

At 328, Corporal Keating and Trooper Vann gave Corporal Bulson and Troopers Falle and Dorn ten seconds to run down the gangway to the side door on the right, before they all break in. Wielding a large wrecking bar, Trooper Vann smashes the front door once, and then raises it to strike again, when the door is suddenly opened from within. James Vann finds himself face to face with a very surprised-looking uniformed Hudson patrolman, while Corporal Keating, hearing the crashing of glass, runs around to the side in time to catch five men climbing out a window.

At the back door, Corporal Bulson tries knocking, but when no one answers he strikes hard with his sledgehammer, knocking out the upper panel. Trooper Falle jumps through and immediately takes off, chasing a black woman he sees running in the long, narrow building. Bulson attempts to follow Falle, but becomes stuck tight in the hole, and Trooper Dorn has to push him through with his foot, causing Bulson to fall in a heap inside.

Trooper Falle rounds up the black woman, apparently a maid, and the men he finds sitting around the kitchen table littered with clamshells and coffee, and herds the protesting crowd into the front parlour. Meanwhile, on the second floor, Mae Healy, who at the first sound of the raid had bolted up the stairs, frantically routs her girls out of the arms of their customers, shoving them in the direction of their hiding place, as she hurries to her own room, anxious to get there before anyone else. From behind her door, she can hear shouting voices and Falle pounding up the steps, followed by the other Troopers who had finally extricated themselves from the wreckage.

All they find are five closed doors and several men in the hallway, trapped like rabbits in a cage. Leaving others to deal with them, Falle and Bulson head for the third floor, but are blocked by a trap door, bolted from above. As they try to get through, Mae Healy kneels in her bedroom, shoving papers and stacks of one and five dollar bills into the space under the floor. She has just risen from replacing the triangular piece of floorboard concealing the cache, when a trooper bursts into the room.

At the top of the stairs, Falle and Bulson have just managed to force the locked trap door, and rush through the opening. There they find an open, attic-like space, still bearing the scars of the fire that had taken place nearly fifteen years before. An old man feigns sleep on a mattress, and hiding behind the joists are three young women, wearing nothing but panties and trying to look nonchalant. As the four are placed under arrest and taken back to the second floor to find the women some clothes, one of the girls remarks, "You know, we haven't seen so many good-looking men in months."

Falle and Bulson take everyone down to the front parlour, adding them to the shouting throng seeking release from Trooper Vann. He, however, is trying to determine exactly what a Hudson police officer is doing in the whore house. Vann knows that the entire local force was to have been detained at the police station as the raid began, but perhaps this man has somehow eluded the net. The Hudson officer says that he was "investigating a noise," having been in the alley at the rear as the State Police broke in. Trooper Vann can't remember having seen him before, but as all is in confusion around him, there isn't time to make judgments. Taking down the officer's badge number, James Vann lets him go, but then another man pushes forward, demanding his freedom as well. He also claims to be a Hudson policeman, but since he is dressed in civilian clothes and not carrying his badge, Vann orders him back inside with the others. The man becomes irate, "Goddamnit! Let me out!" he shouts. "I'm an officer of the Hudson Police Department!" James Vann is not impressed. As the unidentified gentleman stews in the parlour with the dozen or so others, the telephone rings. Corporal Bulson finishes depositing the last of his captives and picks up the receiver to hear the operator say,

"Albany calling. Go ahead, please—35 cents." At the sound of Bulson's voice, the person on the other end says, "Who's this?"

"One of the Troopers," Bulson replies.

There is a pause, then, "Never mind, operator, I don't want this number," and the caller hangs up.

Sergeant Carl Wichmann tours the broken houses, checking to see that his men have everything under control. He inspects each one, walking through all the rooms himself, collecting lists of the occupants and prostitutes' "service cards," making sure that nothing and no one has been missed. Twenty minutes after the raid began, he walks through the front door of 328 and is immediately assailed by a man sitting among the detained people in the parlour, "There's Wichmann! He knows who I am!" Sergeant Wichmann looks over and recognizes a Hudson police officer in civilian clothes. Without comment he confirms his identity and the man leaves in a hurry. Wichmann is too busy to reflect on the reason for the officer's presence as he tours the house and then crosses the street to 325.

The circus continues. Mae Healy gets into a heated argument with Corporal Keating, insisting that she be allowed to leave someone behind to safeguard her property, but her request is denied as the other troopers commence the evacuation of the prisoners. Those detained are loaded into the trucks and taken off to the police station a block away. Bored-looking prostitutes and highly embarrassed johns are deposited in front of the century-old brick building, as a rapidly growing crowd of Hudson residents jeers and whistles. Over 300 people eventually gather, making the event into something resembling a twisted Hollywood opening, each familiar new arrival eliciting a roar from the assembly.

The felons from 7 South Front Street are hauled in. The troopers had been searching for the rumored million-dollar floating crap game, and had reliable information that major underworld figures and stacks of cash would be found. The darkened store was stalked and raided with even more vigor than the houses on Columbia. Seven men were discovered playing pinochle. The troopers arrested them anyway.

Inside the police station, chaos reigns. Desk Sergeant Finck is overwhelmed by the dozens of detainees, until state troopers finally take stacks of arrest forms and sit down to help him process the paperwork. District Attorney McLaren and City Judge Connor make harried arrivals and dive into the morass. One woman says she is a schoolteacher from Albany and was merely visiting her sister who happened to work in a whore house. Some arrested black women insist they were only cooks and maids. The girls brought in from 340 and 344 are grilled as to the whereabouts of their missing madams. A rumor goes around that cars full of disheveled people were seen careening into a gas station north of town. "Hudson's being raided!" they reportedly shouted. "We have to get out!" One man is found to have a gun and is immediately sequestered by the troopers. A lawyer shouts at anyone within earshot on behalf of his clients. Mae Healy faints dead away and a doctor is hastily sent for. The captured johns wait uneasily in a group until they are all dismissed with no charges brought. However, the women are all photographed and fingerprinted before being taken off to jail, to be held until it is determined if they have V.D. The

Hudson police stand in the background, largely excluded from the action, indignant at the outsiders usurping their power. At 1:15 a.m., the man who hosted the pinochle game comes before Judge Connor. By now, the Albany press has arrived, and the poor fellow has the honor of being the only person arrested that night to have his photograph appear in any newspaper. He pleads guilty to being a common gambler and is released after paying a $100 fine. A reporter for the Albany *Times Union* pens this verse as he waits for the gambler's fate to be decided:

> 55 Troopers, axe and gun,
> Went to Hudson on the run.
> Looking for some floating games—
> All they found was painted dames![2]

Back on Columbia Street, the doors to six houses stand splintered and open. A person or persons enter the dark, empty house at 328 and stealthily climb the stairs. Carefully, they check each room behind the five doors lining the second floor hall until they find the bedroom belonging to the owner. The quiet of the night is disturbed once again with the sounds of ripping and breaking, as unfamiliar hands destroy everything visible in the feeble illumination of a flashlight. Two hundred and ninety dollars is found in a nightstand. A bank book is discovered in a drawer. Some framed, personal photographs are removed on a lark. Finally, a foot disturbs a loose, triangular-shaped floor board, revealing a hole underneath. Over three thousand dollars is greedily pulled out of its secret resting place and shoved into a bag. Footsteps are retraced, down the stairs and out the door. Next stop, 340.

All charges are dropped against two women who worked as maids, and the schoolteacher from Albany goes home with lots of explaining to do. In a couple of days, Vera Faith turns up and is promptly arrested. She had been undergoing treatment in an Albany hospital at the time of the raid and had missed all the fun. Before being brought before the judge, however, she has time to discover hundreds of dollars and her bank book missing from her house at 340 Columbia. Mae Healy returns home to 328 after a few days in jail and finds her place totally ransacked. Furniture is destroyed, mattresses and upholstery slashed, and, of course, her money and bank book are missing, along with pictures of her son in his army uniform. Eventually her bank book is returned to her, but she never sees the cash or photos again. Vera Faith, it turns out, has lost even more, namely $20,000 that had been in her savings account. The 50-year-old woman goes into a spasm of very public hysterics, accusing everyone from the state troopers to her own daughter for her loss. Her lawyer starts raising a fuss when suddenly both she and Mae withdraw their charges and even issue stiff apologies. No one ever explains why.[3]

The girls in jail wait two weeks for the results of their blood tests, only to discover there is no infection among them. They are permitted to leave town unmolested if they plead guilty to vagrancy, although one makes a formal request to stay in Hudson because it is her hometown. Five women are convicted of keeping houses used for "lewdness, assignation, and prostitution," defined as places where "the common fame and general reputation of the frequenters and people who reside and who inhabit the aforesaid house is that of being

175

prostitutes, vagrants, and immoral persons."[4] All that verbiage to say "madam." The five ladies are fined $500 and banished from Hudson, although as six houses were busted, one operator seems to have eluded capture altogether. The fact that none of the johns are ever charged escapes everyone's notice except for the Executive Committee of the Hudson Council of Church Women, who express their opinions in a delicately genteel letter to the *Daily Star* dated June 25:

> Through your columns we would like to convey our appreciation to all responsible for the recent efforts towards the eradication of crime and degradation in our community. It was a good beginning. We cannot help wondering why the names of the fifteen [undoubtedly more] men involved were not made known. If it were not for such men, there would be no such business in our city.

John McLaren is left with the unenviable task of explaining to the public and Hudson's power structure exactly what his role was in all this confusion. Basically he says that the Governor's office had received "several complaints" concerning activities on The Block, and that he, as the Hudson district attorney, had been called in secret to prosecute them. The Hudson police had not been used, McLaren stated, because it was feared they could not be trusted to keep the raid secret. Rumors on the street, however, range from Governor Dewey's presumed desire to use Columbia Street to win political brownie points to that of a local gambler encouraging the state authorities, angry at a political system that accepted pay-offs from prostitutes while harassing him.

Whatever the truth, John McLaren is definitely caught in the middle.

Some in the little city hold their breath as they wait for the turmoil to show signs of dying down. Rumors have been flying about the two Hudson police officers found at Mae Healy's as they are suspended pending a departmental hearing. The girls have not reappeared and the houses remain closed. Actually, several of the "escapees" turn up at the knitting mill in Philmont looking for jobs the day after the raid, apparently destitute and not even having been able to change their clothes since being so rudely turned out of their homes. A supervisor is told to see what she can do with these new arrivals, but she is dubious that the woman wearing a tight black dress with the slit up the side will be of any use. After a male employee recognizes one of the girls, the women are fired on the spot. No one has seen them since.

Tuesday, July 18, 1950. At three o'clock this hot, summer afternoon, the state troopers make another Hudson appearance, this time raiding gambling joints all over town. Some of the veterans of June 23 are back, seizing gaming equipment and arresting eleven people, including Benny Goldstein, owner of a local taxi company and organizer of the numbers rackets known as the "Hudson Numbers" and "Catskill Numbers." More arrests follow in the coming days, and now the popular topic is gambling. The newspapers report what was common knowledge. Every business in the county, it seems, can write "policy slips," and even the paper boys put a nickel down on their favorite combination, hoping to win a few dollars. Daily at five o'clock in the afternoon, people from all over dial 555 to reach Black Taxi and the winning number. There are places to bet on the horses, too, Dillon's and Mahota's concealing big, smoke-filled rooms where national race results are received by ticker-tape and posted on blackboards. The national press gets hold of the news, and Walter Winchell dubs Hudson "a little Las Vegas" in his nationwide broadcast. The "million-dollar" floating crap game still eludes detection, but Hudson's power structure begins to crack.

Three days later, the head of the police commission disciplines the Hudson officers found at Mae Healy's. For their "alleged misconduct and incompetency,"[5] one is demoted, the other suspended without pay. Nine days after that, the police commissioner himself resigns, followed immediately by the Mayor. The commissioner states that he didn't realize being a commissioner would take so much time, while Mayor Klein, who has been in office barely six months, cites business reasons. His friends, however, know his frustration at not being able to do anything about the corruption around him, and understand his decision to climb out of the whirlpool while he still can. Exactly one day after the departure of Klein, the two disciplined police officers are exonerated of all blame and restored to their previous positions. The reconstituted police commission states that all evidence against them was merely hearsay. And even though another Columbia Street bordello is raided and closed, it seems only a matter of time before the business climate will return to normal.

A year goes by. John Kelly, determined to reform the system, is elected Mayor. A like-minded Dr. Roger Bliss becomes police commissioner. And Governor Dewey's New York State Crime Commission, under the direction of

Judge Joseph M. Proskauer, has just finished exposing official corruption on the docks of Brooklyn. Now they are directed to peel the lid off the City of Hudson, and they do so with vengeance.

December 19, 1951. A parade of witnesses, including just about everyone in Hudson with a position of authority on either side of the law, is dragged through the courthouse to speak of things usually left unspoken. Madams talk of friends in high places, bribes left in envelopes, and demands for porterhouse steaks. When pressed to explain the nature of her business, Carol Desmond replies, "Well, the girls embroidered, crocheted—they sold things."[6] A "service card" filled with heart-shaped punches along with a payment schedule is displayed. The reporter for *The New York Times* hisses to the woman sitting next to him, "I don't care how illegal it is. I have to get my hands on that punch!"

Taxi drivers recall picking up police officers and prostitutes at whore houses and taking them to dance halls.[7] But the police officers, when grilled by Judge Proskauer and his investigators, recall nothing at all.

> Q. You saw men going in and out of these houses of prostitution, didn't you?
>
> A. No, sir.
>
> Q. I thought you told us you had a beat on that block more than once.
>
> A. Oh, I've been detailed down there, sure.
>
> Q. You mean, to stand in front of the place?
>
> A. No! Walk back and forth!

Q. You never saw anybody going into those houses?

A. No, sir. I never did.

Q. Have you normal eyesight?

A. Yes, sir. I think so.

Q. With glasses?

A. With glasses.

JUDGE. They seem to have done a pretty good business according to the report of this landlady. [Desmond] Apparently everybody could see it but the police officers of the city of Hudson![8]

A police veteran of 31 years testifies that he has never made an arrest for gambling or prostitution.[9] Another states that there were implied instructions to "lay off" the vice merchants.[10] Yet another denies ever having even heard of the prostitution in town.

The frustrated questioners continued:

Q. Did you ever see an unusual number of men congregating around the houses—the so-called houses of prostitution in "The Block"?

A. I never seen them congregating around the houses. I seen them walking through the street.

Q. Did you ever question any men walking through the street?

A. No, I didn't....

Q. Did you do any law enforcement work at all?

A. Yes.

Q. What arrests did you make? Do you remember?

A. Passing traffic lights.

Q. Did you make any arrests other than for traffic violations?

A. Yes. I did make a gambling arrest.

Q. When was that? Do you remember?

A. `51

Q. How many?

A. One.[11]

It becomes more than evident that the patrolman on the street was merely acting according to long-established custom, set up and enforced by his superiors. A former police commissioner is slowly roasted over coals:

> Q. Wasn't it common gossip and a matter of some notoriety around Hudson for many years that "The Block" was almost wide open?
>
> A. Well... the question... to discuss it... that was the Chief of Police, and every time he went through "The Block"...
>
> JUDGE. Come on! Answer the question! Was it common gossip and rumor that "The Block" was operating for many years up until the time you became the police commissioner?
>
> A. I believe so. You're right.

Q. And I want to know what you, as police commissioner, did about it.

A. I reported it to the chief of police.

Q. What did he do about it?

A. I believe he went over there himself.

Q. And what did he report back to you?

A. That he went there himself.

Q. To investigate, you mean.

A. To investigate.

Q. And did he make reports back to you on what his investigation showed?

A. Well, maybe not at that time. Maybe a day or two later...

Q. What would the reports show?

A. That the places were closed.

Q. The places were closed up?

A. That's right.

JUDGE. For how long? Fifteen minutes?

A. That I couldn't say.

Q. What would happen when you would get more complaints that they were opened up again?

A. The same routine again.

Q. With the same result?

A. That's right.

Q. And that kept going on, over and over again, during the years that you were police commissioner? And you fell for that?

A. Well, I wasn't down there too much. I don't think I spent... Well, I...[12]

The huge scope of the gambling operations is revealed, with ties to everyone from New York City crime syndicates to Western Union, which provided the ticker tapes that connected Dillon's and Mahota's horserooms to racetracks around the nation. It is revealed that the basement of the Oneida Food Market was one of the main accounting centers for the illegal betting operations. The names of many prominent citizens are mentioned time and again as key gamblers, the recipients of pay-offs, or the actual owners of raided Columbia Street properties. They staunchly deny any knowledge of what their tenants were up to. Various officials have been required to fill out financial statement forms, detailing their income and expenditures in the years before the raid. A good number seem to have spent more than they earned. [13]

A young lawyer from New York City describes the floating crap game, which drifted from restaurant to taxi office to auto body shop, operating long after the raids in the summer of 1950. He tells of 50 to 75 players a night betting upwards of $300 on each toss of the dice. He tells of cars being sent to New York, Pittsfield, and Schenectady specifically to pick up groups of gamblers waiting at pre-arranged sites, and of "Connecticut Joe," who brought people up on the train. He tells of borrowing money "from the house" at 30 percent interest, and of embezzling his clients' funds—a small amount at first, then thousands and tens of thousands of dollars—all to be lost on a gaming table in a little upstate town, until at last he is reduced to begging for $5.00 to pay his train fare home. And finally, he tells of his arrest and imprisonment at Sing Sing for his sins. "I thought that I could be the exception to the rule that gamblers have to die broke... I was like a madman."[14] The "million-dollar" floating crap game, in fact, netted something like $70,000 a month, but eventually floated away before any of its major organizers could be caught.

The local officials of both political parties, several of whom are current or former police commissioners or county sheriffs, discuss passing out one and two dollar bills on election day, for "political purposes." "Don't use the phrase 'political purpose'," Judge Proskauer shouts, "because that's an insult to politics!"[15] The path of bribe money from prostitutes to political coffers is gradually wormed out of the reluctant witnesses. The elaborate maneuvers to find malleable mayoral candidates are detailed.

And finally it's District Attorney John McLaren's turn to defend his actions. Once again, he carefully explains his involvement in the sequence of events leading up to the raid. He relates how, upon taking office, a local racketeer had delivered a "Christmas present" of $100 stuffed in an envelope, assuring him that there would be plenty more if he would just play along, and how he agonized before finally returning it. And he is asked by Judge Proskauer exactly why, as district attorney, he didn't ever go after the political corruption he saw all around him. The witness tries to respond:

Let me just say this. Anything I did against some of the people, I'd go wrong no matter what happened. Some of the names mentioned here, if there is evidence to convict them, then I would be the biggest—excuse the expression—S.O.B. in Columbia County. If I failed to convict them, then I would have laid down on the job because of past friendships or something like that. Now, I have no qualms whatsoever about prosecuting anybody such as the gangsters and racketeers who have been here, but for me... You have adduced evidence here which would tend to indicate that perhaps [the county sheriff] had been guilty of misconduct. [He] has been a close friend of myself and my family for over thirty years. I've gone camping with him...

And then McLaren bursts into tears.[16]

He has revealed the crux of the problem. Hudson is a small town where everyone knows everyone else. The mayor went to school with the cop who married the sister of the lawyer whose wife is the accountant to the businessman. It is a place full of Mom and Pop stores, even if those stores happened to be a whore house and a floating crap game. As in any other small town, the people have grown up accommodating one another, looking after each other's children, helping with household chores, and keeping the state troopers from raiding the neighborhood house of ill fame. It is something that outsiders just can't entirely understand. Then, of course, there is all that tax-free money to be made....

Evidence revealed in the hearings causes the local heads of both political parties to resign and 12 of Hudson's 18 police officers to be indicted on charges of perjury or accepting bribes.[17] One is "permitted" to retire, one pleads guilty to bribery, and two are publicly tried in nasty, contentious actions that take years. Madams and state troopers return to court once again. A former prostitute tries to jump off the roof of the Lincoln Hotel before she testifies about the patrolmen she gave money to.[18] A prosecuting attorney is compelled to resign when it is revealed that he has "wined and dined" Carol Desmond in New York.[19] Mayor Kelly has an armed guard because of threats made against his safety, just as Mayor Klein had been threatened back in 1950 when all this mess began.[20]

There are mistrials, convictions, and appeals. The two officers found at Mae Healy's continue to insist that they were merely "investigating a noise" when the troopers barged in. Although there is much testimony to the contrary, it is all gradually whittled away. Sergeant Wichmann didn't actually see the accused in the whore house before the raid. An old nervous breakdown is dredged up as proof of Vera Faith's insanity. The ex-hooker who tried to kill herself is similarly discredited. And one of the defense lawyers plays heavily on jury sympathies by going on and on about his client's children and aged parents and ruined reputation. His voice is choked with sobs. Anguished tears of compassion stream down his face. Rumor has it that he has concealed a freshly-cut onion in his handkerchief.

The officers are not only acquitted, one of them will eventually be appointed police commissioner. All the rest are subjected to an internal police investigation, which finally announces that "no evidence of wrongdoing" is found before all are restored to duty with back pay and benefits.[21]

A few civilians are convicted on various counts related to gambling, but out of the whole affair, Benny Goldstein is the only person actually to go to jail for long. The popular rumor is that he is the fall-guy for someone far more powerful. Although he is supposed to be sent to state prison, Goldstein never gets transferred out of Hudson and spends one year assigned to a comfortable cell in the jail behind the courthouse, receiving friends, family, and conducting business. "Benny was a helluva nice guy," one man remembers.

The houses are padlocked by order of the district attorney. Although others open sporadically over the years, what everyone knew as The Block is gone forever. The old madams drift away. Vera Faith ends up managing a stationery store in an Albany suburb. Carol Desmond continues her business under a different name, first in New York, later in Syracuse. Mae Gordon lives out her remaining years with her daughter in Albany. And Evelyn White stays on alone at her former Palace of Pleasure in Hollowville, long after its heyday has passed. Years later, one of the neighborhood children who loved her, now fully grown, rings Evelyn's bell, remembering the fairytale Christmas parties of times gone by. An old, decrepit woman finally opens the door and squints at the visitor whom she cannot recall. Through the open doorway, the ex-playground of the elite is visible, shabby and cluttered with newspapers. Dust and cobwebs hang where a naked judge once chased pretty girls for fun.

8: WELCOME TO HUDSON, PART TWO

❖

HUDSON, NEW YORK, JULY 11, 1992. A LIONEL train set meets *Architectural Digest*. The old town hasn't changed much physically in 40 years. Handsome Victorian buildings still line the now brick-tiled sidewalks, their survival due not so much to preservationists' zeal, but to the fact that nobody cared enough to tear them down during the period when they were unfashionable. Now they are all the rage, with more than half the town listed on the National Register of Historic Places. Federal grants were obtained to spruce up Warren Street, *The New York Times* called it a "treasure of architecture,"[1] and hundreds of people pay $10 each for the historic-house tour held every spring. Long-time residents think they're crazy.

Trains still stop at the quaint little station, Promenade Hill still commands a glorious view of the Hudson River, and the miniature metropolis is still largely surrounded by woods and orchards, although just north on Route 9, the enveloping suburb of Greenport has encouraged unregulated commercial development, creating a tangled and growing cancer of shopping centers and fast food. Despite all that, Hudson's downtown has survived better than many facing similar competition.

Some of the old businesses on Warren Street remain. However, Rogerson's Hardware, Sam's Market, and Wolf-Weintraub's paints are now wedged in between hairdressing salons, upscale restaurants, and nearly two dozen antique stores, expensive Empire furniture and styling gel taking the place of Macy's housewares and Hymie Richmann's dresses. The police station and city offices have moved out of the venerable old building with the big auditorium above, but a citizen's group has banded together to raise money for restoration of the space into a civic center. At 1:00 p.m. every afternoon, people gather at the intersection once known as Central Square to buy the first copies of the daily newspaper still printed there. Its headlines trumpet the news on crime ("Erie County Woman Arrested for Giving Unauthorized Enemas") and on health ("Ignorance a Big Complication of Impotence").

The local citizenry enjoy many of the same pleasures that their parents and grandparents did: hunting and fishing in the countryside, as well as swimming out at Spook Rock and boating in the River. Softball and bowling teams continue to be fielded by local businesses as well as every one of the six volunteer fire companies, each of which still maintains its own spotless fire truck and neat, brick firehouse. On weekends one can attend church suppers, dances at the Elk's Club, or lectures at the D.A.R., and nowadays many people flock to one of the numerous country auctions which sport names like "Stuff and Things," where one can buy everything from old cars to oil portraits of Mamie Eisenhower, all for a song or two. And Warren Street continues to host parades, fairs, and running events, although the Soap Box Derby was replaced by bed races some time ago.

A rather strange residential mix has evolved by 1992, a combination of people charmed by the city's beauty, trapped by inertia and poverty, or just predisposed to live in the same place as their ancestors. Well-known artists, teenaged mothers on welfare, television celebrities, retired cement factory foremen, interior decorators, middle-class working people, a Pulitzer Prize-winning poet, farm laborers, antique merchants, drug dealers, lawyers, prison guards, Old Money, and New Money trying to act Old all live as neighbors in their grand or formerly grand houses, in a town seemingly too tiny to contain such diversity.

Hudson's old reputation lives on. When a young sculptor moved here from Connecticut with her husband and daughter three years ago, her 80-year-old father exclaimed, "Hudson? What do you want to go there for? There's nothing but whores!" But Hudson's vice is not quite the same. To be sure, gambling is still here and more open than ever, with Hudsonians regularly betting on the horses and playing the numbers. Now it's mostly through the New York State Lottery and OTB parlours, with Albany taking the profits once pocketed by gangsters and racketeers. However, that hasn't stopped some of the old die-hards from pursuing the illegal, underground buck, with some of the same people arrested in 1950 continuing to be nailed by the State Police, well into the 1990s. Modern judges have been letting them go because of their advanced age.

Prostitution is still here also, although it doesn't remotely resemble The Block of yesteryear. A few sad, emaciated girls turn occasional tricks in order to earn money for drugs, at prices not much higher than those found on Columbia Street in the 1930s. For much poverty can also be found in Hudson, exacerbated by the closing of factories and, it is rumored, by a drive in the 1970s to attract welfare families to town in order to reap profits off Federal grants for subsidized housing. A real-estate boom brought a frenzy of speculation during the 1980s, but then some investors let their greed get out of hand and were burned during a recession in the housing market. The town was burned too, the welfare families and the investors' hoarded buildings left abandoned and forgotten, waiting for a savior.

And yet another political scandal has taken place in Hudson recently. A police chief was indicted on over 20 varied counts of official misconduct when he supposedly blocked state troopers' investigations into the booming local drug traffic. Once again, ugly trials seemed to go on forever, with raging passions and nasty accusations from both sides. Once again, even the national press picked up the story, and once again, Hudson's sordid secrets were exposed to outside eyes. In the end, the Chief was acquitted of most charges on appeal, but not before he lost his job and brought down the somewhat ridiculous mayor who supported him. The police department was reported to be demoralized. It all seemed so familiar, somehow.

Today, however, the community's residents have tried to put that behind them as they gather to watch the annual Fireman's Day parade, supposedly the biggest ever. It is a beautiful summer's day, and bright red trucks and shiny, antique pumpers from all over the state roll majestically down Warren Street, accompanied by marching bands, Ladies' Auxiliaries, and the special float featuring a homemade replica of one of the Proprietors' sailing ships, built for Hudson's Bicentennial in 1985.

William D. Allen, the new reformist mayor, accompanied by his hand-picked police commissioner and police chief, strolls in its wake, waving cheerfully at the eclectic crowd standing in front of the elegant displays in the smart shop windows. The mood is good, but Hudson still squirms a little as it struggles to find a new image to put on over the old. The people smile and wave back, glad to see that their community is improving under new management, but secretly wondering if, deep, deep down, they wouldn't rather return to the bad old days....

Columbia Street, three blocks from the River. It is part of a truck route now, continuing its long tradition of being the place to relegate the noise and smells not welcome in the better neighborhoods. In order to get through town, tractor-trailers must use State Route 9G, which crosses the marsh that was once the South Bay and climbs the steep hill, becoming Third Street in the process. Where it meets Warren there is a traffic light that always seems to be red. So the big rigs wait, their engines idling on the spot where Albert Downing's horse broke from its traces before running up the street and broadsiding a sleigh during that Christmas season in 1876. Charley Hermance took his last drunken walk past this corner, and an hour later, Fidel

Wise streaked by in the opposite direction, panic in his voice as he screamed, "Murder! Murder! I need a policeman!" If the truck driver cares to look to his left, he can see an empty lot bordered by a burned-out building where a frightened Giles Spaulding yelled for the doctor. Look again, and maybe the trucker can see the armor-plated Packard pulled up to the curb, with dangerous-looking men carrying violin cases guarding the unassuming building where their boss is getting a shave and a haircut behind tightly drawn shades.

All around the rig are the sites of former speakeasies where men and women got drunk on homemade hooch, imported whiskey, and once even on a bottle of water disguised as gin. A little further to the right is the apartment where the state liquor agent lived in self-imposed ignorance, and further still is the big brick building where patrolmen were told to stay out of the bootleggers' way.

The light finally changes, and the sixteen-wheeler is coaxed into motion, crossing Warren and continuing down Third where it has to negotiate the tricky right turn onto narrow Columbia Street. The driver is too involved in the maneuver to notice the building formerly housing the Colored Citizens' Club, once the largest black-owned club between New York and Buffalo, standing empty on the corner, waiting for a revival that may never come. Across the street is the empty lot where Arthur Trebilcox's Adirondack Hotel stood until this year, the beautiful young woman who so scandalously danced the St. Louis long since in her grave. The smell of diesel fuel prevents the truck driver from noticing any odor from the sperm oil works that once operated nearby, but then it has been well over 150 years since the last barrel of whale blubber was processed there. However there is still a little grocery on another corner, where prostitutes used to buy vinegar and paper napkins in giant economy sizes, and in front of which an old man looked up and down, up and down before making his twice-weekly dash into the arms of a reluctant paramour.

The tight turn has finally been accomplished, scattering any cars foolish enough to pull in front of the stop-line, purposely placed well back to give the trucks some room. The huge engine roars into life as the machine passes through what was once The Block, drowning out any echoes from more than 150 licentious years. An aging Chevy van sits in the muddy yard at Kate Best's former place of business, where one should be able to hear the riotous mob who came to seize her husband in 1869. Across the street, a newly built house occupies the site where girls were paid to scream and scream at a strange man sitting in a coffin, and at one of the shabby street's now empty lots, perhaps one can just make out the voice of a man shouting, "I'm paying a dollar a shot and she's drinking *tea*!"

The truck roars along The Block, much as the police cars and paddy wagons did on a warm Friday night five years after the War. It follows Columbia out to Green Street and the road leading north, retracing the path of a couple of speeding, bulbous sedans, full of half-dressed people shouting, "Hudson's being raided! We have to get out!"

The driver is too young, too preoccupied to have noticed the ghosts, the shadows of people leaping from the windows of the little houses, with other shadows chasing them to and fro, like some strange dance in a dream. There a young man watched his life and career evaporate with the roll of the dice, a woman watched her daughter recoil from her in shame and disgust. There played out the passions of lust, of murder, of greed, and sometimes of humour and happiness. The air whispers of the past, but most people are deaf to Spirits. What were those sounds, that sighing to be heard after the truck had finally gone? Was it the wind in the trees, the creak of a shutter? Or was it the sound of dozens, no, hundreds of women's voices echoing in the air: "Wanna make a baby? Wanna make a baby? Wanna trip around the world?"

NOTES for Chapter One

1. All events are taken from the pages of the Hudson *Daily Star* and an interview with "Paul Cocheran."

NOTES for Chapter Two

1. Some authors accept the Jackson White legend as fact, others are not so sure. See *City of Eros*, p.24; *Great River of the Mountains: The Hudson*, p.41.
2. *Hudson Directory, 1871*, Introduction.
3. Hudson *Balance and Columbian Repository*, March 3, 1807.
4. *The Administrative Effects of the Breakdown of Law Enforcement in Hudson, New York*, pp.56-58.
5. Cleanliness: an On-again, Off-again Practice, *Smithsonian*, February, 1991, p.134.
6. *City of Eros*, p.69.
7. As late as the 1920s, it would have been possible for the City of Hudson to simply annex Greenport without a public referendum, thus with the stroke of a pen restoring Hudson's tax base and ability to expand. This course of action was proposed in 1923, but was roundly defeated for unknown reasons. The state laws concerning annexation were soon changed, and Hudson missed her last opportunity to free herself easily from Greenport's stranglehold, about which people still loudly complain 70 years later. See *The Administrative Effects...*, p.47.
8. Minutes of the Common Council, Hudson, July 25,

1843. (according to Mary Wend)

9. Columbia County *Washingtonian*, July 20 and July 27, 1843.

10. Minutes of the Common Council, Hudson, July 25, 1843. (according to Mary Wend)

11. Hudson *Evening Register*, August 7, 1869.

12. In 1888, Hudson's house-numbering system changed. 165 Diamond became 325 Diamond. Still later Diamond became Columbia.

13. According to Hudson's first anti-vice ordinance enacted May 26, 1859, keepers of brothels or gambling houses could be fined up to $25. Owners of buildings where such activities took place could receive a similar fine. Common gamblers or prostitutes could be fined between $5 and $25.

14. Ulster County Court Proceedings, "People vs. Conroy," as reported in the Hudson *Register*, January 18, 1877.

NOTES for Chapter Three

1. The events and dialogue related in this chapter are taken from the Hudson *Register*, December 20, 1876—January 2, 1878, which includes testimony from the Grand Jury hearing, December 26, 1876, and trial testimony from February, 1877. As with any major event, witnesses' recollections differed in many details. I have sifted through all the versions and tried to come up with the most logical narrative.

2. Hudson Common Council Minutes, February 1, 1877.

3. Although the newspapers would refer to her as 16 or

"in her sixteenth year," later testimony revealed that she was in fact 15, having been born in June of 1861. Her marriage took place when she was 14.

4. The Kieres' brothel was in the Second Ward (the area north of Warren, bordered by Third and the River), Hudson's poorest neighborhood. According to census records, 33 people died natural deaths there between June 1, 1874 and June 1, 1875. Their average age was 19. Even excluding the 19 children under 15 years old, the average age at death was only 43, the most common causes being tuberculosis, cholera, "inflammation of the bowels," "water on the brain," and something called "inanation." By contrast, the upper-middle-class First Ward (the neighborhood on the other side of Warren, bordered by Third and the River) saw 17 deaths during the same period, with an average age of 49. Excluding the three children in that number, the average age rises to 59. Further exclude the young woman who died in childbirth at age 23 and the 19-year-old boy who succumbed to "gastric fever," the average rises to 66. Nine of the 17 who died in the First Ward were over 60. Only 5 of the 33 in the Second Ward had reached that age.

5. When the 1875 Census was taken, on June 1, 1875 Irene was 17. So by Christmas of 1876, she would have been 18 or 19.

6. For more on nineteenth century prostitutes' earnings, see *City of Eros*, Chapter 3.

7. Hudson *Register*, February 13, 1877.

8. *Ibid.* February 21, 1877.

NOTES for Chapter Four

1. All events for 1877 were taken from a daily reading of the Hudson *Register*, March 1—December 31, 1877, unless otherwise noted.
2. *The Administrative Effects of the Breakdown of Law Enforcement in Hudson, New York*, p.66.
3. *Ibid.*, pp.30-32.
4. Hudson *Evening Register*, September 23, 1869.
5. *The Administrative Effects of the Breakdown of Law Enforcement in Hudson, New York*, p.31.
6. *Hudson City Directory, 1871*, Introduction.
7. *The Administrative Effects of the Breakdown of Law Enforcement in Hudson, New York*, p.58.
8. Hudson *Republican*, August 3, 1887.
9. Hudson *Register*, September 19, 1877.
10. Hudson *Register*, October 10, 1882.
11. *The Administrative Effects of the Breakdown of Law Enforcement in Hudson, New York*, p.71.
12. Hudson Common Council Minutes, January 1, 1894.
13. Hudson *Republican*, May 2, 1908.
14. *The Administrative Effects of the Breakdown of Law Enforcement in Hudson, New York*, pp.74.
15. Hudson *Evening Register*, August 10, 1901.
16. *Ibid.*
17. Hudson *Republican*, July 26, 1901.
18. Hudson *Evening Register*, August 1, 1901.
19. *Ibid.*, August 8, 1901.
20. Mayor Van Hoesen, Common Council Minutes, May 1, 1912, May 1, 1913.
21. Hudson *Evening Register*, March 18, 1912.
22. *The Administrative Effects of the Breakdown of Law*

Enforcement in Hudson, New York, pp.82-83.

23. Common Council Minutes, February 26, 1920; April 19, 1920.
24. Hudson *Register*, June 25, 1920.
25. Mayor Glaster, Common Council Minutes, May 2, 1922.
26. According to Officer Joseph Pazera, who joined the force in 1923, Hudson *Register-Star*, August 4, 1954.
27. Hudson *Republican*, October 29, 1921.
28. Grand Jury "Report on Vice Conditions in Hudson" to Judge Daniel V. McNamee, March 8, 1931.
29. Officer Joseph Pazera and others in Hudson *Register-Star*, August 4, 1954.
30. Columbia County Court records, "People vs. Kane."
31. According to R. W. Herzberg, Hudson *Register*, September 9, 1938.

NOTES for Chapter Five

1. Most information for this chapter comes from dozens of interviews with current and former Hudson residents who worked both inside and outside The Block.
2. N.Y. State Crime Commission Hearings, Hudson, December 19, 1951, Transcript pp.545-46.
3. According to Pauline Tabor, *Pauline's*.
4. Hudson Police Blotter, 1949, March 3.
5. *Ibid.*, March 3.
6. From Robert Mitchell's interview with Bart Delaney Sr., Hudson *Register-Star*, May 26, 1991.
7. Hudson *Daily Star*, July 2, 1939.

NOTES for Chapter Six

1. Unless otherwise noted, information in this chapter comes from interviews with those who worked or played in the Houses on The Block, all of whom request anonymity.
2. According to inventory in Mrs. Church's will, filed July 5, 1939.
3. N.Y. State Crime Commission Hearings, Hudson, December 19, 1951, Transcript p.564-66.
4. *Ibid*. pp. 558-562.
5. *Microbe Hunters*, The Magic Bullet, p.366. I also use information found in a coverless, and therefore, anonymous sex-manual found among a Hudson Madam's papers, circa 1920.
6. From a collection of a madam's papers found in a former whore house.
7. *Ibid*.
8. *Ibid*.
9. *Ibid*.
10. N.Y. State Crime Commission Hearing, Hudson, December 19, 1951, Transcript p.568.
11. Columbia County Court Records.
12. A madam's papers.
13. *Ibid*.
14. *Ibid*.
15. *Ibid*.
16. Hudson *Register-Star*, July 30, 1954.
17. Hudson Police Blotter, 1949, April 29.

18. Hudson, *Register-Star*, August 4, 1954; also Crime Commission Transcript, pp.643-47.
19. Columbia County Court Records.
20. Crime Commission Transcript, pp.559-60.
21. Hudson *Evening Register*, January 16, 1953.
22. Crime Commission Transcript, pp.555-57.
23. Survey of Commercialized Prostitution Conditions, Hudson, New York, June, 1950.
24. *Ibid.* see also *Look Magazine*, "A Look at Sin," February 26, 1952.
25. A madam's papers.
26. *Ibid*.

NOTES for Chapter Seven

1. Information in this chapter is assembled from interviews with witnesses and testimony at the Crime Commission Hearings, pp.656-73, and accounts in the Hudson *Evening Register, Daily Star* and (after 1953) *Register-Star*, the Chatham, N.Y. *Courier*, the Catskill, N.Y. *Daily Mail*, the Albany, N.Y. *Knickerbocker News* and *Times-Union*.
2. Albany, N.Y. *Times-Union*, June 25, 1950.
3. Hudson *Evening Register*, September 30, 1950 and January 16, 1953.
4. Columbia County Court Records.
5. Hudson *Evening Register*, July 24, 1950.
6. N.Y. State Crime Commission Hearings, Hudson, December 19, 1951, Transcript, p.566.
7. *Ibid.* pp.547-49.
8. *Ibid.* pp.620-21.

9. *Ibid*. pp.846-47.

10. *Ibid*. p.856.

11. *Ibid*. pp.634-36.

12. *Ibid*. pp.527-29.

13. *Ibid*.

14. *Ibid*. pp.725-40.

15. *Ibid*. pp.521-23.

16. *Ibid*. pp.872-90.

17. That is, 12 of the 18 on the force in 1950. By the time the indictments were handed down in 1952, the police department had 21 members.

18. Hudson *Register-Star*, July 15, 1954.

19. Chatham, N.Y. *Courier*, January 23, 1953.

20. Hudson *Daily Star*, May 9 and September 30, 1952.

21. Hudson *Register-Star*, October 8, 1954.

NOTES for Chapter Eight

1. *The New York Times*, "Summer Slice of Life Up the Hudson," July 20, 1989.

2. Headlines from the Hudson *Register-Star*, 1986, 1990.

BIBLIOGRAPHY

BOOKS:

Adler, Polly, *A House is Not a Home*. Rinehart, New York, 1953.

Bettman, Otto L., *The Good Old Days—They Were Terrible!* Random House, New York, 1974.

Bowen, Croswell, *Great River of the Mountains: The Hudson*. Hastings House, New York, 1941.

Gilfoyle, Timothy J., *City of Eros: New York City, Prostitution, and the Commercialization of Sex, 1790-1920*. W. W. Norton & Co., New York, 1992.

de Kruif, Paul, *Microbe Hunters*. Harcourt, Brace & Co., New York, 1926.

Lant, J. H., *Hudson Directory, 1871*, "Introduction." Reissued privately by Barbara Mazur, Hudson, 1985.

Manners, Dorine, *Scarlet Patrol, My Story*. Godwin, New York, 1936.

McMullin, Jean Brice, *Hudson Revisited*. Hudson, N.Y., 1985.

Tabor, Pauline, *Pauline's*. Touchstone, New York, 1971.

Various Contributors, *Columbia County at the End of the Century*. The Record Printing and Publishing Co., Hudson, N.Y., 1900.

Wend, R. Mary, *The Administrative Effects of the Breakdown of Law Enforcement in Hudson, New York, a Thesis*. Presented to the Graduate School of Public Administration, New York University, June, 1963.

REPORTS AND COURT RECORDS:
Census Records, Columbia County, 1855 – 1950.
Columbia County Court Proceedings.

Columbia County Probate records.

Common Council Minutes, Hudson, New York.

Grand Jury Report to Judge Daniel V. McNamee, March 8, 1931.

Hudson, New York City Directory, 1851 - 1952.

Hudson, New York Police Blotter, 1949.

Hudson, New York Property Maps, 1801 – 1875.

New York State Crime Commission Investigation. First Report to the Governor, the Attorney General, and the Legislature of the State of New York, January 23, 1953.

New York State Crime Commission, Public Hearings, Columbia County, Transcript December, 1951.

Report to Governor Franklin D. Roosevelt, February 27, 1930.

Report to the Governor on Social Evils in Syracuse, New York, 1912.

Survey of Commercialized Prostitution Conditions, Hudson, New York, June, 1950 and August 1950, prepared by the American Social Hygiene Association.

MAGAZINES AND NEWSPAPERS:

Albany, New York, *Knickerbocker News.*

Albany, New York, *Times-Union.*

American City, August, 1949, March, 1961.

Catskill, New York, *Daily Mail.*

Chatham, New York, *Courier.*

Columbia County, *Washingtonian.*

Hudson, *Balance and Columbian Repository.*

Hudson, *Daily Register.*

Hudson, *Daily Register-Star.*

Hudson, *Daily Star.*

Hudson, *Evening Register.*

Hudson, *Evening Star.*

Hudson, *Register.*

Hudson, *Register-Star.*

Hudson, *Republican.*

Intermountain Express, January 19, 1979

Journal of Social Hygiene, 1948-51.

"A Look at Sin", *Look,* February 26, 1952.

The New York Times.

Stuller, Jay, "Cleanliness: An On-Again, Off-Again Practice" *Smithsonian,* February, 1991.

PLUS:

Private Papers of a Hudson Madam.

Photo Archive of a Hudson news photographer, courtesy of Bruce Bohnsack, Germantown, New York.

Photo Archive from Rowe's Studio, courtesy of Hudson Public Library.

Video Interviews on file with RSVP, Hudson, New York, courtesy of Marchella Beigel.

Personal interviews with current and former residents of Hudson, ex-bootleggers, ex-gamblers, ex-racketeers, ex-steerers, ex-johns, ex-girls, and others who witnessed The Block from both inside and out (including the man who said, "Just because I'm old doesn't mean I know anything about history!"), who shall remain anonymous at their request.

INDEX

Abortion: 27, 150-151, 153

Adirondack Hotel: 66-67, 193

Albany, N.Y.: 12, 30, 50, 58, 70, 73,
116, 140, 152, 155, 165, 173,
175, 187, 189

Allen, Rev. (Pastor, Shiloh Baptist
Church): 113-114

Allen, William D. (Hudson
Mayor): 192

American Legion: 3

American Social Hygiene
Association: 164-165

Anti-Rent Wars: 20

Architectural Digest: 188

Arkinson, Police Officer: 117

Arkison, Police Commissioner: 65

Athens, N.Y.: 2, 4, 14

Batchellor's Fancy Goods Store: ii,
34

Bars (see Saloons)

Beecher, Charlie: 166-167

Belmont, Betty: 126

Bennet, Julia: 63

Benson, Dr.: 46, 193

Benson, Mrs.: 5, 118

Benton, Harriet ("Hat") and
household: 26, 55, 62

Berman's Furniture: 1, 131, 155

Best, Archibald (Hudson Mayor): 74

Best, George: 21-24, 31, 41, 123, 194

Best, Kate: 21-24, 54, 115, 123, 141, 194

Big Bridget: 21

Big Charlie: 161

Big Mae: 124

Big Minn: 124-125, 161, 163

Birth Control: 150

Black Taxi Co.: 177

Bliss, Dr. Roger: 178

the Block (see also Brothels,
Madams, Prostitutes, Prostitution,
Hudson Streets, Red Light
District and indiv. names):
business fluctuations; 21, 36, 116,
119, 152, 164, 167, 191, 194
children's attitudes towards;
117-118, 120, 122-123, 127-128,
134-136, 187-188
in decline; 163-165, 168, 169,
187
descriptions of; (18th Century)
15-16; (19th Century) 25-26;
(1930s, 40s, 50s) 6-8, 9-10, 73, 75,
76, 112-125, 130-131, 151, 155;
(1990s) 194-195
and holidays; 123, 128, 152, 187
and the law; 22-23, 62-64, 74-76,
117, 168-183, 187
"legitimate" businesses on; 6,
15-16, 114, 127, 193, 194
and out-of-towners; 13, 56, 116,
117, 118, 120, 183-184
and V.I.P.s; 73, 116, 122-123
working population; 164

Bonaparte, Napoleon (letter to
Josephine): 16

Bootlegging and Bootleggers: 68-
70, 75, 154, 193

Boston, Mass.: 2, 140

Brace, Mary (see Nell Weeks)

Brancari, Andrew: 33

Brancari, Irene: 30, 31, 33, 36, 37,
38, 39, 40, 41, 42, 45, 46, 48,
50, 41, 53, 198

Bristol, England: 11

Brothels:
addresses of; 21, 32, 41, 62, 66,
75, 115, 120, 122, 123, 124, 125,

207

ABOUT THE AUTHOR

Before Bruce Edward Hall became a writer, he had another career as a puppeteer in both television and film, having appeared as everything from Miss Molly's goofy helpers in television's long-running *Romper Room*, to Fozzie Bear's girlfriend in *The Muppets Take Manhattan*, to a love-sick Dolphin opposite Jean Stapleton and Rue McClanahan in *Let Me Hear You Whisper*. He has also worked as an actor on both stage and screen.

As a writer, Mr. Hall has contributed numerous feature articles to *The New York Times*, *New York Magazine*, *American Heritage*, and *Christopher Street*, among others. While Diamond Street is his first book, his short story, *Ghosts*, will be in *A Reader's Repertoire*, to be published by Harper Collins in 1995.

Through A Woman's Eye, Pioneering Photographers in Rural Upstate, by Diane Galusha. Turn-of-the-century rural America as it was seen and experienced by three farmers' daughters who became pioneering photographers in the remote northwestern Catskill Mountains. They became the principal chroniclers of their communities, preserving for all time images of a bygone world, affording the modern viewer a window on the past through the unique perspective of a woman's eye. 200 pages, 61 full page photographs, paper, $29.95.

The Old Eagle-Nester, The Lost Legends of the Catskills, by Doris West Brooks. Nominated for a national story-telling award, *The Old Eagle-Nester* combines fiction and legend with a "pinch of magic and a smidgen of witchcraft." *"A beautifully designed and illustrated book,"* said the *Hudson Valley Literary Supplement. Dutchess Magazine* proclaimed, *"This is wonderful stuff, some of it funny, some of it frightening, all of it entertaining."* 128 pages, illustrations, paper, $13.95.

The Mill on the Roeliff Jansen Kill, by The Roeliff Jansen Historical Society. From its founding in 1743 by the Livingston family, through 250 years of Hudson Valley history, the story of the oldest operating commercial mill in New York State, a collaborative work by seven historians, was recognized by a joint legislative resolution by the Senate and Assembly of New York State commemorating this publication. 144 pages, 36 photographs, 2 maps, paper, $15.00.

Chronicles of the Hudson, Three Centuries of Travel and Adventure, by Roland Van Zandt. From Robert Juet aboard the Half Moon in 1609, to Henry James's reflections as he viewed the Hudson through the windows of a steam engine train in 1905, Van Zandt captures 300 years of travelers' adventures and perspectives in this "journey through time." Hudson Riverkeeper John Cronin, in his introduction notes: *"Each generation born to the Hudson is entitled to its own journey of discovery. Roland Van Zandt's legacy to us is as a friend and tour guide on that journey."* 384 pages, 51 illustrations & maps, paper, $24.95.

Kaaterskill, From the Catskill Mountain House to the Hudson River School, by the Mountain Top Historical Society. The legendary Kaaterskill—synonymous with scenic beauty; inspiration for Thomas Cole and the Hudson River School; the birthplace of American mountain resorts; immortalized by James Fenimore Cooper and William Cullen Bryant; and now the heart of the Catskill Park and Preserve—profiled from seven different perspectives by seven prominent authors. 120 pages, 30 illustrations, hiking map, paper, $13.95.

Big Hollow, A Mountaintop History, by Elwood Hitchcock. An intimate portrait of an isolated mountain valley community that witnessed the changing fortunes of the Catskills in microcosm; from wilderness to a scattering of family farms, through the "grand hotel" era, to the modern day— a return to quiet farms and country retreats in the shadow of a decaying resort, all amid the splendor of a hiker's paradise of thousands of acres of forest preserve. *"If there is such a thing as 'living history,' Mr.*

Hitchcock and his book are it." *(The Advocate)* 128 pages, 25 illustrations, paper, $14.95.

A Catskills Boyhood, My Life Along the Hudson, by Philip H. DuBois. An octogenarian professor emeritus recalls a bucolic childhood growing up in one of the oldest villages along the banks of the Hudson River, watching the advent of the modern age as the horse and carriage gives way to the Model-T. *"This book is filled with fascinating tidbits of life in the early century." (Kingston Freeman)* 128 pages, illustrations, paper, $12.95.

Mountaintop & Valley, Greene County Folk Arts Today, by Field Horne. Forty-eight folk artists profiled and photographed—from quilters, fish net weavers and stone wall builders to the "cutting edge" of chain saw carvers. Artists profiled were selected for the dignity and quality that their art presents, and the resulting book was awarded the coveted Heritage Award from the Federation of Historic Services. 48 pages, 33 photographs, paper, $10.00.

Books available from the publisher:

BLACK · DOME

Black Dome Press Corp.
RR 1, Box 422
Hensonville, NY, 12439
Tel: 518 734-6357 Fax: 518 734-5802
Prices & availability subject to change.